REGNUM GLOBAL VOICES

The Good News of Creation

Series Preface

The **Global Voices** series takes the missiological work of writers who have written in their own language and makes this accessible to the English-speaking world through translation and republishing. The key principle here is that the translated work reflects the context, experience and thinking of the local context. In so doing, Regnum Books seeks to amplify voices less easily heard outside their own contexts. Work of this nature will make a significant contribution to the development of 'polycentric missiology'; namely, mission thinking and practice that truly reflects the contexts, concerns and contributions of the global church in all its rich diversity.

Series Editors

The Good News of Creation
Eco-theology for Faithful Discipleship

Juan Stam

Translated from the Spanish by Daniel Clark

Edited by Mark Greenwood

First English edition published 2023 by Regnum Books International
The original edition by Juan Stam was published in Spanish
by Nueva Creación, a division of William B Eerdmans

Regnum is an imprint of the Oxford Centre for Mission Studies
St. Philip and St. James Church, Woodstock Road
Oxford OX2 6HR, UK
www.regnumbooks.net

British Library Cataloguing in Publication Data

A catalogue record for this book is available from the British Library

ISBN: 979-8-8898-3309-3
eBook ISBN: 979-8-8898-3310-9

Typeset by Words by Design

Cover image by Hanson Lu on www.unsplash.com

i

The publication of this volume is made possible through the financial assistance of Evangelisches Missionswerk.

Distributed by Fortress Press in the US, Canada, India, and Brazil

Dedication

For Manuel Figueroa,
a pastor at heart, a profoundly biblical preacher,
a tirelessly researching thinker, disciple, pilgrim,
faithful until death;

and for René Padilla,
pioneer amongst Latin American Theologians who seek to
love God with all their mind, brave and tenacious prophet
of the integral gospel of God's kingdom and his justice.

Contents

Contents

Foreword to the English Edition

Juan Stam's Impact within the Integral Mission Movement
Tim Carriker

The original proponents of the Integral Mission movement are commonly identified as Carlos René Padilla from Ecuador, Samuel Escobar Aguirre from Peru and Carlos Caldas Orlando Enrique Costas from Porto Rico. Their participation and especially the presentations of Padilla and Escobar in the first International Congress on World Evangelization in Lausanne, Switzerland in 1974 mark a particular milestone for the movement. The general idea within the Evangelical movement that evangelization and social transformation are symbiotically integral to the church's mission was already highlighted in 1966 at the Congress on the World Mission of the Church in Wheaton, Illinois, in contrast to the World Congress on Evangelization held in Berlin, Germany the same year. The emphases of these two world congresses of Evangelicals highlighted the tensions among Evangelicals that continue today, concerning the proper role of social transformation within the mission of the church. Padilla, Escobar and Costas made a decided stand for the integration of the two and the subsequent Lausanne Covenant confirmed and legitimized their approach.

In the following years other important Latin American leaders became associated with Integral Mission: Plutarco Bonilla Acosta from Spain and Costa Rica; Pedro Arana Quiroz from Peru; Edward Robinson de Barros Cavalcanti, Valdir Raul Steuernagel, Carlos Pinheiro Queiroz and Jorge Henrique Barro, all from Brazil; and Juan Stam from the USA and Costa Rica. Other worldwide church leaders gave their support as well, notably: John Stott from the U.K., and Vinay Samuel from India. Among all these, Juan Stam particularly stood out.

I first met Juan Stam in Brazil in the early 1980s and was immediately impressed by his disarming jovial manner, his political transparency (he was wearing a Sandinista T-shirt) and his keen biblical and theological bearings. He was already well known as a sort of fourth pillar of the integral mission movement alongside René Padilla, Samuel Escobar and Orlando Costas. Except for his tall, lanky physique, everything else pointed to a thoroughly Latin American persona. How could this be, and what were Stam's particular contributions to the movement?

The institutional connection with the integral mission movement came through Juan Stam's tenure on several faculties in Costa Rica. Plutarco Bonilla had been Professor of Philosophy at the University of Costa Rica from 1962 to

1991 and Academic Dean and Rector at Seminario Bíblico Latinoamericano. Orlando Costas also taught at SBL from 1970 to 1974 where he worked with International Institute of In-Depth Evangelism (IINDEF), became active in the Latin American Theological Fraternity (FTL) in 1972, was elected as their Executive Secretary in 1977 and founded the Latin American Center for Pastoral Studies (CELEP) in 1973. These institutions formed a sort of nest for the development of the integral mission movement, and in the middle of them was the widely recognized, bright, jovial, American-Costa Rican. Juan Stam had served on the faculty of SBL from 1957-1980, the National University of Costa Rica from 1974-1994, and afterwards served on the faculties the Seminário Teológico Bautista in Nicaragua (1981 to 1985), the Seminário Nazareno de las Américas in Costa Rica (1990-1995) and the Universidad Evangélica de las Américas (UNELA) in Costa Rica (1992-2002).

Juan Stam was someone of outstanding academic credentials, a deep, personal faith in Jesus Christ and equally deeply committed to an evangelization that transformed not only personal lives but also permeated and demanded the transformation of social structures. Deeply rooted in evangelical faith and trained at the best North American evangelical institutions at the time -Wheaton College (B.A. and M.A.) and Fuller Theological Seminary (B.D.) with George Ladd - Stam's early commitment to an incarnational approach to mission drove him to pursue further studies at the Universidad de Costa Rica in literature and philosophy and eventually doctoral studies under Karl Barth and Oscar Cullmann at the University of Basel in Switzerland, and post-doctoral studies in Tübingen, Germany under Hans Küng and Jürgen Moltmann. In each of his degree studies, Juan was at the top of his class.

But Juan, true to his pietist, evangelical upbringing, considered the Bible his first book, whose ultimate authority demanded interpretation as-free-as-possible from tradition, including the evangelical tradition. That stance nudged him initially towards neo-evangelical leaders such as Berkouwer, Ladd, Ramm, Carnell and Jewett. While teaching a course on The Church and Society in the late 1950s and early 1960s, Stam was particularly impacted by the witness and examples of Dietrich Bonhoeffer, Martin Luther King and Nelson Mandela, and soon afterwards, Helder Cámara and Oscar Arnulfo Romero. Later influences came from Kierkegaard, Barth, Brunner and Tillich as well as René Padilla, Samuel Escobar, Pedro Arana, Roland Gutiérrez and José Miguez-Bonino.[1]

Stam considered himself to be a "radical evangelical" in the sense of being driven constantly to the roots of his faith in biblical teaching. In 2018 the Catholic priest, Miguel Picado Gatjens, described Stam as a "free theologian" in that same sense of independence from any one interpretive school.[2]

Stam was someone ripe for the integral mission movement and he dove headfirst into it, not only through his own pastoral ministry during his years of tenure as seminary and university professor as well as through numerous trips

[1] http://eric-cunha.blogspot.com/2014/02/adelante.html.

[2] https://www.informa-tico.com/10-08-2018/juan-stam-teologo-libre.

sponsored by Centro Evangélico Brasileiro e Ecumênico de Pastoral (CEBEP) and other organizations throughout Latin America and especially Cuba, where he led theological retreats for pastors and church leaders. He was also a constant figure and speaker at the continental wide Latin American Congresses on Evangelism (CLADE) promoted by the FTL (1969, 1979, 1992, 2000, 2012).

Finally, as other Latin American Integral Mission theologians, Stam leaves a lasting legacy through his writings. Besides the hundreds of articles, Stam has written a number of important books. Probably the two farthest reaching are this current volume, for its genuine originality and ground-breaking, biblical breath, and his massive four volume[3] commentary on Revelation: *Apocalipsis: Comentário Bíblico Iberoamericano* (I in 1999, II in 2003, III in 2004 and IV in 2014). The latter was his life-long passion, especially relevant for its prophetic contribution to social transformation. His more general *Escatología bíblica y la misión de la iglesia* (1999, 2001) provides the necessary interpretive tools behind Stam's approach.[4] And so, while theology and history are the primary tools for the development of integral mission by René Padilla, Samuel Escobar and Orlando Costas, Stam complements that approach in constant dialogue with both biblical passages and a social analysis of Latin American. Beginning initially with an exposition of the Bible to elaborate a theological approach, he then applied this to an evangelical vision for the transformation of Latin America's diverse contexts.

---

[3] Over 1,500 pages.

[4] Guatemala, Semilla 1999 (2nd Edition, Quito, CLAI, 2001 and a 3rd edition as *Profecía bíblica y la misión de la iglesia*, Havana, Cuba).

Preface

This work emerged as I authored various essays over a two-year period. As the essay drafts developed, they acquired a coherent structure so that I felt compelled to unite them in a single book, published with the prayer that it may help edify those belonging to our Lord and Creator.

Early in 1991, the coordinating commission of CLADE III assigned me to speak on "The Gospel of the new creation." This suggestion came at an opportune moment, encountering fertile soil as I have spent years studying the book of Revelation and relating it with Genesis and creation theology. The theme immediately fascinated me and allowed me to reflect on a vital theme for our understanding of all of Scripture and especially the book of Revelation.

All Clade III presentations were sent to participants and to the national and regional cells of the Latin American Theological Fraternity, prior to the consultation in Quito in August 1992. I received almost a hundred valuable responses from brothers and sisters from all over the continent. Edesio Sánchez and José Enrique Ramírez, both Old Testament specialists and valued colleagues over many years offered valuable suggestions.

During the months of preparation for CLADE III in Quito, immersed in the riches of the biblical theology of creation, I received an invitation to take the Manuel Figueroa Chair at the Instituto Teológico Bautista de Santa Ana, El Salvador. This provided me with the opportunity to reflect further on other aspects of this theme. Manuel Figueroa, a friend for many years, had died at a noticeably early age, victim of a cancer which quickly reaped his promising life. He was a dynamic pastor, and I had the personal blessing and joy of preaching many times at his congregation, the First Baptist Church of Santa Ana. Manuel, a philosophy teacher at the Baptist College in Santa Ana was a true theologian and philosopher. My conversations with him concerning our faith and the meaning of our discipleship would always lead me to be enriched in Christ and discover something new about the truth. Furthermore, over the years, Manuel introduced me to a deeper understanding of the realities of Central America and his beloved country, El Salvador. We would often discuss the book, journals, and articles he recommended. Therefore, I dedicate this book, along with the Santa Ana conferences, to the memory of such a unique companion in the struggle for the gospel.

The final preparations for CLADE III led to a better elaboration of the meaning of the biblical creation theology for our complex contemporary world.

These materials are present in the last chapter, which retains the talk's original format. In this chapter I analyse themes such as human dignity, the rights of each person independent of race, sex, social or economic condition, our ecological responsibility and our Christian commitment to justice and reconciliation in favour of an authentic *shalom,* in the light of creation and new creation. I have sought to emphasise that the Bible has much to say to us today with regards to these themes, and others of ethical importance.

Creation theology should play a decisive role in our understanding of the gospel, of mission, the church, and our faithful discipleship as the first fruits, here and now, of the new creation. I am convinced that this should be an integral part of the biblical and theological renaissance Latin American evangelicals desire. I hope with all my heart that these pages may contribute to this end, for the glory of the Word through whom all things were made, who became flesh and in whom all things will find their final consummation.

Introduction

A comparison between the first page of the Bible (Genesis 1:1) and the final page (Revelation 21:1ff) reveals that the theme of creation is a decisive axis in biblical thought. The Bible's whole message is developed between two creation narratives, from Genesis 1:1 "In the beginning, God created the heavens and the earth", through Isaiah 65:17, "for behold I create new heavens and a new earth", until Revelation 21:1 "Then I saw a new heaven and a new earth." The first narratives reveal God's purposes for his creation. It is no mere coincidence that the terminology is the same, apart from one basic difference: the adjective "new." This clearly indicates that the Bible narrates the movement from the original creation until the final creation which will consummate God's redemptive action.

All sections of the Bible, from start to finish, tell us about creation. In these pages we will try to explore the wealth of biblical creation theology and the role this can and should have in our thought and action as contemporary Latin American evangelicals.

Biblical teaching on creation is not restricted to the first chapters of Genesis, as many seem to think, nor does it take the form of a single, static, fixed formulation. It is a concept which grows and develops over the centuries, using different expressions and images and goes through surprising transformations in its meaning. In this dynamic process, the theme of creation is always linked inseparably with the development of the biblical message of salvation.

The Bible's compressive emphasis on creation indicates that this is a central theme in its message. If our salvation culminates in this promise of new heavens and a new earth, then this hope should decisively shape both the message and the mission of the church. For this reason, this book's thesis is that *there is no healthy biblical and evangelical missiology without an adequate creation theology.*

Evangelical theologian Bernard Ramm has expressed the vital nexus between creation and mission:

> It is in creation theology that we find the definite root of a theology of evangelisation … We can only evangelise with moral integrity when we have a deep theology of evangelisation and this theology of evangelisation begins with a creation theology (1978:1; cf. Padilla 1986:3, 10ff).

Ramm's starting point is the difference between evangelisation and proselytism, and whether an evangelist can rightfully claim to have a unique and divine message. Can we dare to do this with integrity? Ramm points out, through Jonah's example, that the prophets preached at a time when Israel lacked prestige as a nation. The fact that Yahweh was the creator of the entire world gave them the authority to prophesy to any nation in the world and all peoples. These prophets affirmed that God, as creator and judge of all nations, had sent Assyria and Babylon to punish Israel for its sins. As Yahweh was the God of justice over all nations, they understood his power in increasingly universal and cosmic ways (cf. Moltmann 1969: chapter 2). God sends his messengers to all creation, not because his people have superior qualities when compared to other people, but because all the universe is rightfully his through creation and redemption.

Mervin Breneman, in a valuable series of articles in the *Misión* journal, has pointed out that the foundations for mission lie in creation. "God's creation of the entire world and all of humanity means that all must submit to his sovereignty (Psalm 24:1-2; Ephesians 3:8-11)" (1886:75). Breneman comments that the prophets declare that God is sovereign over the history of all nations, so that God's people have the responsibility to take the word of the Lord to all nations on the earth (1884:28).

Bertil Ekstrom from Brazil, in response to my CLADE III presentation, correctly points out that in cross cultural situations such as Lystra and Athens, Paul started his evangelisation with creation. In *El llamado ineludible* (1969), Kenneth Strachan proposed that our participation with our neighbour in a common humanity created in the image and likeness of God is the fundamental starting point for evangelisation.

Our purpose is therefore to trace the development of the theme of creation throughout Scripture, to discover the extent of its message and the impact of its demands for the life and mission of our Lord's church.

Creation and Salvation in the Old Testament

Our understanding of creation, as with other biblical teachings, tends to be very distant from biblical thinking. This distortion can be attributed to different causes:

1) An exclusive focus on Genesis 1-3, divorced from other texts concerning creation and the promised new creation.
2) Creation is misunderstood as a static concept rather than a dynamic reality in constant development and change.
3) Genesis 1-3 is interpreted within our modern scientific mentality rather than the prescientific reality and issues of its own time.
4) Genesis 1-3 is read exclusively as an antievolutionist polemic.
5) We divorce creation from salvation, whereas biblical thinking understands creation in the light of salvation and salvation from the perspective of creation.

These traditional errors need to be overcome to understand creation biblically. We need to carefully and faithfully seek the authentic exegetical message of each of the key texts from Genesis to Revelation. We also need to capture the theological dynamic that emerges as this teaching develops progressively. Finally, we need to reconceptualise salvation, mission, and evangelisation in the light of a better understanding of this decisive ingredient in biblical teaching.

Creation and Salvation in Genesis 1-3

Genesis' creation stories are not primarily concerned with the origin of things but the meaning of creation and God's purposes for human life. Genesis 1 does not describe how God brought things into being out of nothing but how he separated them, ordered, and filled them, culminating in his own image and likeness in human beings. Genesis 2:4b-25 presupposes the existence of the world and narrates, in an extraordinarily beautiful manner, the progressive humanisation and socialisation of our existence and subsequently its dehumanisation through sinful rebelliousness.

It is important to recall that all the Pentateuch, including Genesis, was written *after* and in the light of the redemptive experience of the exodus, as a commentary on this divine gesture of salvation. The light of salvation is projected backwards from the exodus to find its prehistory in the patriarchs and even in the origins of "the heavens and earth" and of life. The God of the exodus is also the God of creation and of the fathers; the God of creation is none other than the God of salvation and history.

The obvious conclusion is that the creation narratives themselves were written with a salvific historical intention. This intention is revealed in important aspects of Genesis 1-3. For example, the divine word and the weekly structure which culminates in the sabbath just as God spoke to Moses from Sinai and ordered the consecration of the seventh day. God is the sovereign Lord of the world and of history, the only actor in creation and salvation who creates freely, with no previous material, and likewise sovereignly and freely chooses Abraham and Sarah to create a family line through pure grace and divine power. God also freely chooses and redeems his people in the absence of any prior merit or efficacious cause in us (Deuteronomy 7:7). The narratives of Genesis 1-3, in their historical context, reveal a clear salvific sense to creation and prepare the scene for the future history of salvation (cf. Genesis 3:15). The evangelical theology of grace begins with Genesis 1 (Losada y de Angulo 1992: 17-43)!

The verb "create" (*bara*) refers to divine action, without effort or resistance, without helpers or rivals, which produces something new which only God can carry out. God is the only subject of this verb in all the Old Testament. Beyond the creation of the world (Isaiah 40:28), its use outside of Genesis 1 describes a wide range of divine creative actions:

A. The creation and redemption of Israel as a people (Isaiah 43:1, 7, 15),[5] and the "creation" of the covenant (Exodus 34:10).
B. Israel is created again in salvation (Isaiah 45:8, 4:5, cf. Habakkuk 3:13; Jeremiah 31:22).
C. The creation of each person (Isaiah 54:16, Psalm 89:47; Malachi 2:10).
D. The creation of a new heart in each repentant sinner (Psalm 51:10, cf. Isaiah 57:18).
E. The creation of new events, both good and bad (Numbers 16:30, Isaiah 45:7ff; 65:18; Jeremiah 31:22).
F. The creation of new heavens and new earth (Isaiah 65:17ff: 66:22).

The semantic range of *bara* and its synonyms leads to the conclusion that the correlation between creation and redemption in a salvific-historical sense is being revealed from Genesis 1 onwards. The Creator of the universe also creates salvation and life for his people.

Likewise, the use of the expression "generations" (*toledoth,* 2:4a) for God's divine action in Genesis 1 also links creation directly with the first stages of salvation history narrated in the rest of the book. Genesis repeats nine times, at decisive points, the identical phrase "these are the generations of" (6:9; 10:1; 11:10,27; 25:12, 19; 36:1, 9; 37:2). This formula, with its allusion to biological procreation, fits seamlessly with texts describing human descent and the

---

[5] Cf. *Asah* (make) and *yatsar* (form) in 43:21; 44:2, 21, 24, 45:11.

historical narratives of the history of the patriarchs. Nonetheless, "generation" does not easily fit the creation of the world by God's sovereign word. Likewise, the plural formula (generations) fits perfectly in the other passages where it is used, but it would be contradictory to interpret Genesis 1 as a series of births. These apparent anomalies indicate that the use of *toledoth* in 2:4a reflects the author's desire to link his creation account with the subsequent narratives. The author seems to be signalling that creation is the beginning of the subsequent "generations" of salvation history.

It is noteworthy that the formula "these are the generations" appears at the end of the creation account (2:4a) whereas in the rest of the book it always comes at the start of a new section (6:9, for example). In other passages the formula introduces the subsequent narrative, but the creation account has a separate introduction (1:1); so that the formula functions as a conclusion in 2:4a. This detail suggests that the end of creation, God's rest, is the start of salvation history.

Genesis insists emphatically that creation is *good.* The phrase is repeated, rhythmically, as the dramatic conclusion to each day. Human creation, including sexuality, and all God's work is "very good" (1:31, *tob tob).* The goodness of physical creation is central to the message of Genesis 1: matter and the world are a blessing not a curse. The Old Testament rejects any dichotomy between spirit and matter, between a good soul and an evil body.

Eugene Peterson aptly emphasises that "creation submerges us in a principle of materiality" (1988:170). This same materiality will be key for the biblical message of salvation: in the incarnation the word became matter, *sarx,* (John 1:14), Jesus's physical death redeems us "in his flesh" (for example Colossians 1:22, Ephesians 2:15, Romans 8;3, 1 Peter 3:18; 4:1); and our hope lies in Christ's bodily resurrection and our new body (Luke 24:37-43). Our salvation has a deep material dimension, faithful to the ancient affirmation of the goodness of creation and the rejection of any dichotomy between spirit and matter.

The meaning of the adjective "good" is not only ethical, but also aesthetical as God's world is a successful artistic creation, and functional for what was created fulfils divine intension effectively. It communicates a playful tone: God stops to contemplate his creation and feels content; he rejoices in the excellence of what he has done (cf. Proverbs 8:30ff; Ruiz de la Peña 1986:55; Anderson 1984:15). The black poet James Weldon Johnson captures this beautifully in his poem *Creation* from *God's Trombones:*

And God stepped out on space,
And he looked around and said:
I'm lonely—
I'll make me a world.
...
Then God smiled,
And the light broke,
And the darkness rolled up on one side,
And the light stood shining on the other,
And God said: That's good!

...
Then God walked around,
And God looked around
On all that he had made.
He looked at his sun,
And he looked at his moon,
And he looked at his little stars;
He looked on his world
With all its living things,
And God said: I'm lonely still.

Then God sat down—
On the side of a hill where he could think;
By a deep, wide river he sat down;
With his head in his hands,
God thought and thought,
Till he thought: I'll make me a man!

This great God,
Like a mammy bending over her baby,
Kneeled down in the dust
Toiling over a lump of clay
Till he shaped it in is his own image;

Then into it he blew the breath of life,
And man became a living soul.
Amen. Amen.[6]

Many biblical passages on creation reflect this celebratory note and sense of joyful adoration. This blissful tone reveals how liberatory the biblical message of creation was in its context compared to other mythological cosmologies. John Driver emphasises that in other ancient cultures the world was a source of fear and one had to carry out rituals to protect oneself. In contrast, Driver indicates that the Bible teaches that creation is good for all, including animals; it is not "good for some and evil for others" (1991:15, cf., Losada y de Angulo 1992:19-22).

The adjective "very good" (1:31) strongly emphasises the superlative excellence of human creation in God's image and likeness. The superlative in 1:31 stands out even more in the solemn, liturgical style of the chapter. Auzou calls it a "challenge to pusillanimity" (1982:285 quoted in Ruiz de la Peña 1986:42). Consequently, a biblical faith can never be misanthropic or dehumanising. Biblical faith is a courageous affirmation of the dignity of human

[6] The whole poem is ten verses long and offers an enchanting Afro-American version of creation. In *Zorba the Greek* Katzanzakis gives us a pleasing Greek version: after creating Adam God does not see clearly what he has created, and Adam looks like a pig. However, God soon puts on his glasses and says, "It is good."

beings and therefore of the seriousness of sin and all injustice which harms and damages persons.

The expression "image" also emphasises the materiality in biblical thought. Outside of Genesis it refers to a carved image (Numbers 33:52; Daniel 2:31-35; etc), or a painting (Ezequiel 23:14). Human beings, in their physical corporeality and sexuality, are a visible representation of God on earth.[7] In the ancient world the expression "image of God" was also used to describe kings; in Egypt Pharoah was considered the "image of God living on earth" (von Rad 1982:68ff quoting WH Schmidt). Von Rad also points out that ancient kings used to erect images of themselves in each imperial province to represent their power and authority and power over the region (1988:71; cf. Driver 1991:14). In contrast, God has raised his image in his created realm: us!

Genesis 2:4a-4:25 is even more explicit than Genesis 1 in the way that it links the narrative of human origins with the subsequent history of sin and salvation; it is all told as part of one continuous narrative. The story of Adam and Eve does not take place in some mythological or divine territory but is roughly located within the known geography of its time, in Eden, close to the sources of the Euphrates (2:8, 14). The narrative also emphasises the links with the ongoing human drama. After creation in Eden, the narrative moves on seamlessly to the rupture caused by initial sin (Genesis 3), Cain's fratricide and the origins of human civilisation (Genesis 4), the judgement through the flood (Genesis 6-9) and the call of Abraham and Sarah (Genesis 12:1-3). Creation's meaning is obviously inseparable from the narrative of sin and salvation.

Chapter 3 introduces disobedience (verses 1-16) and the consequences which will affect the future of humanity (verses 7-24). Nonetheless, amid this announcement of how life will be under sin (the curse of verses 14 and 17) we have the proclamation of a struggle throughout generations (verse 15, "between your offspring and her offspring") and the mysterious promise of the triumph of the woman's seed (verse 15 "he shall bruise your head"). Human generations continue in chapter 4 from the Stone Age to the Bronze Age to the Iron Age, in the history of cities (verse 17), civilisation (verse 22) and culture (verses 21ff), yet, while music and culture emerge, the moral deterioration caused by sin never ceases.

Although Genesis 2:4a-3:24 is a simple narrative, it has a surprising and impressive historical perspective for such an ancient text. Its horizon is that of "the Palestinian peasant established on the edge of the desert" (Guelley, 1979:48). It describes the process of forming the peasant world in three stages:

A. From the arid desert to the fruitful garden: 2:4-17.[8]
B. From the plant to the animal kingdom, agriculture to zoology and cattle raising: 2:18-20.
C. From loneliness to marriage, individualism to community: 2:21-25.

---

7 See John 1:14 "we saw his glory". Von Rad comments that since creation the glory of God "clearly has human contours" (1972:195; cf. Ezequiel 1:26; John 1:14).

8 See later Canaan where "milk and honey flow".

The disobedience in Genesis 3 introduces two further stages:

D. From harmony to sin; the fall: 3:1-13.
E. From sin to salvation, a long struggle between the woman and the serpent (cf. Revelation 12): 3:15, 12:1ff.

Genesis 2-3 describes *Yahweh Elohim* as a "working God". God "formed" *(yatsar)* Adam, "sowed" *(natac)* the garden and "built" *(banah)* Eve from Adam's bones. These three terms are nearly always used for human beings, especially roles such as potter, sculptor (Isaiah 45:9; 64:8), farmer and carpenter.[9] The verb *yatsar* is used various times to describe God's salvific work: God "forms" Israel (Isaiah 43:21, 44:1ff, 24, cf. 27:11). *Natac* can also have a salvific meaning: God "sows" Israel (Jeremiah 2:21; 11:17).[10] In other passages *banah* refers to Israel: God promises to build a house and a throne for David (2 Samuel 7:27, Psalm 89:3ff): later, God promises to rebuild the people upon their return from exile (Psalm 102:16ff; 147:2).

W. Foerster (1965: 1007-1010) provides many examples of the artisan God in the Old Testament. The Creator "stretches out the heavens like a curtain and spreads them like a tent to dwell in" (Isaiah 40:22, cf. 44:24, Zechariah 12:1). He made the skies "hard as a cast metal mirror" (Job 37:18). As an architect or builder, God built the world on columns (1 Samuel 2:8, cf. Psalm 93ff, 96:10, 104:3). Other passages describe creation as a weaving (Job 10:11, Psalm 139:13, 15) and a birth (Psalm 90:2, Job 15:7, cf. Romans 8:22). E. Schillebeeckx (1977:506) summarises this theme with an analysis of four ancient versions of creation: 1) work, 2) procreation, 3) struggle and 4) speech.[11]

In the original Hebrew Genesis 2-3 includes a series of wordplays which are both aesthetically pleasing and thematically significant. Of these, three are particularly important for the original author:

1. In 2:7 the author states that from the earth *(adamah)* God made *adam:* the *adamah/adam* wordplay strongly establishes the inseparable and essential link between humans and the earth between *homus* and *humus*. In a quite different way from the first chapter, we have a new and dramatic insistence on materiality, which will characterise all of God's plan for salvation.
2. The second wordplay emphasises the mysterious and deep solidarity between ish (man) and ishah (woman) (2:23) inseparably united in a common life.
3. There is also a wordplay between Eve *(javah)* and living *(jayah)* in Genesis 3:20.

---

9 W. Zimmerli (1980:33). "All these terms come from the spheres of gardening and craftmanship and are usually used to describe human activities." Cf. Schökel 1969:28.

10 In 31:28 it describes restoration as a salvific act.

11 See the note on Genesis 2:7 in the Jerusalem Bible. León Durfuor 1965-1970 and the section below on "creation and environmental stewardship".

Despite human disobedience, God remains faithful to his promise of life and salvation for Adam, formed from *adamah,* and the woman made from the man (*ish).*

These chapters emphasise that God has made us for communion. Leslie Newbigin, in *Sin and Salvation* (1956) points to the network of harmonious relationships which Adam and Eve lived in before sin: God with Adam and Eve, Adam with Eve, humans with the land and animals. Newbigin affirms that the fall led to alienation in all these relationships including with oneself (cf. Driver 1991: 15-16), and Anderson (1957:169) declares that "rebellion against God is rebellion against our very own humanity." Yet, within the narrative of the fall there is the beginning of the promise of integral salvation. God made us from the earth and sin returns us to the earth, but by his own grace God will once again breathe life within us and we will be, in Christ, "recreated after the image of the one who created us" (Colossians 3:10).

The missionary message of the Bible has its roots in these chapters. Mervin Breneman reveals the impressive universal focus of Genesis 1-11, to the extent that these chapters do not even mention typically Jewish themes such as Palestine, Israel, and Jerusalem. "God is the Creator and Lord of everything … God is interested in all the nations of the world" (1984:28). For Breneman, "the biblical doctrine of mission is not based on a few isolated passages but rather on a focus which is present throughout all the Old and New Testaments, starting with the universal focus of Genesis 1-11" (1982a:26, cf. 1982b:22ff).

Creation and Salvation in the Poetic Books

Rather than being restricted to the first chapters of Genesis, the theme of creation runs through the whole Old Testament, usually in direct relationship with God's salvific action. This rich creation theology confirms our thesis: the Old Testament understands God's creative activity as good news. We will try to briefly summarise what the poetic books, Psalms and Songs of Solomon, and the wisdom books, Job, Proverbs and Ecclesiastes, teach about this theme.

While some Psalms worship God for creation in itself (e.g., 8, 19, 104), most poetic and wisdom passages integrate creation and salvation in one single divine salvific act (Psalm 33; 74:12-17; 89:5-18; 136). According to Psalm 89 creation is the beginning of "the steadfast love of the Lord" (89:1, 14). Similarly, Psalm 139 extols God's mercies (verses 1-3) in creation (verses 4-9) in the exodus (verses 10-22) and his constant protection and nurturing of all that breathes (verses 23 to 26). The exodus is experienced once more in the continuous rescue of the faithful (verse 24); and creation is experienced in the "food to all flesh" (verse 25) given by "the God of heaven" (verse 26). In this way, this beautiful liturgical psalm links creation with past and future redemption.

Poetic and wisdom literature describes creation in diverse, occasionally surprising ways. Its original and distinctive contribution is the concept of creation through Wisdom (Proverbs 8:22-26; 3:19, cf. Sirach 24:1-29, Wisdom of Solomon 7:22-8:1). But, whereas in Genesis 1 God speaks to create, in these passages Wisdom is alongside God as a "master workman" (Proverbs 8:30), when God constructed the world, shaped the mountains, made the earth and its fields, drew a circle on the face of the deep, established the heavens and assigned to the sea its limit (Proverbs 8:25-30). In a comparable way Job 26:7-14 describes creation as a construction (cf. 38:4-7, Psalm 104:2-5) and binding the threatening waters, by decree, with bars and doors (cf. 38:8-11).

Job 26:11-14, as can be discerned in the more accurate translations, adds a third theme: creation as a victory over the primitive monsters, Rahab, Leviathan, and the tortuous serpent (cf. Job 7:12, 9:13; Psalm 74:12-17; 89:9ff; cf. Genesis 1:21; Isaiah 27:1). In these poetic descriptions, creation is perceived as a dramatic struggle and divine triumph over the forces of chaos and evil. This soon becomes translated into a double symbol of creation and exodus, as Rahab is also associated with the Nile. Psalm 104:26 even includes the Leviathan within the good creation of God, as the monster "you formed to play." Here, rather than a terrifying threat, the monster is God's pet and play companion. These ways of conceiving creation, so different from the first chapters of Genesis, corroborate the theological relationship between creation and salvation.

Creation and Salvation in Isaiah 40-66

The prophetic books are extraordinarily rich in creation theology. Jeremiah affirms divine creation of the earth, which grants God the full right to distribute it as he wishes (27:5). For Jeremiah, Yahweh, as Creator, is the legitimate sovereign over the nations and history. Jeremiah also emphasises that the reality of creation guarantees the order of nature, the seasons of the year, day and night, rainfall, and harvest (5:24, 14:22, 31:35ff; cf. Genesis 8:22). The universe's faithful rhythms are based on the covenant between God and creation (Genesis 9:8-17), which confirms the faithfulness of God's covenant with his people (Jeremiah 33:20). Jeremiah also announces a new covenant, which is the foundational contract for the new creation, as occurred in the first creation (cf. Hosea 2:18); and the creation of a new heart, the inner force of the new humanity (Jeremiah 36:31; cf. Ezequiel 36:26). As for Amos, he directs three doxologies towards the creator (Amos 4:13, 5:8ff, 9:5ff) and Habakkuk includes a long prayer full of creation theology (Habakkuk 3:1-9). In Jonah, as already indicated, we find a missiology based on faith in creation.[12]

Nonetheless, no biblical book is more important than Isaiah in developing a theology of creation. Chapters 40 to 66 refer continuously to creation, with the regular use of verbs such as create, make, and form. These chapters reach the peak of Old Testament creation theology and introduce the revolutionary concept of a new creation.

These chapters also emphatically accentuate the salvific meaning of creation. Yahweh, Lord of the universe, "Creator of the ends of the earth" (40:28) is also

[12] More details on creation in the prophets can be found in Schökel-Sicre, 1979 and von Rad, 1973.

Lord of his people, "Creator of Israel" (43:15), Lord of history, the creator of salvation and justice (45:8) and Lord of the future, creator of the "new things" such as the return to Canaan, messianic salvation and eschatological fulfilment which will bring Israel liberation (48:6ff; cf. 42:9, 43:18-21). The great acts of salvation that God will carry out will also be acts of creation (41:17-20; 45:1-8; 48:6ff).

When faced with the despair of exile, the prophet does not base his eloquent message of new hope on abstract principles but turns to Israel's salvation history. His constant paradigm for the promised salvation is the exodus, which originally delivered Israel and made it into a people.[13] Restoration will be a new exodus which will surpass by far the first liberatory experience.

Yet the author takes a further step, perceiving both the first and the promised second exodus, the return, as new manifestations of God's original creative act. God's redemptive power displayed in the exodus and in history was already manifest in the original creation so that now, exodus and restoration, Messiah and eschaton are all new recapitulations of the first act of creation. Hermeneutically, the prophetic interpretations of all these past and future acts are impressive new readings of the original creation paradigm. Creation, exodus, the return from exile, the future hope for the suffering servant and the new creation cannot be understood separately, they are meaningless on their own. The first or ancient things, creation, and exodus, are the hermeneutical key for the new things which God announces through his prophet.

The theme of creation dominates Isaiah 40-45. In his initial poem, the author proclaims the evangelical consolation of God's creative work (40:12-17, 21-31). Creation is linked with a strong polemic against idolatry (40:18-20). Once again, the theology of creation becomes the missionary motivation to proclaim the good news of the creator (40:3, 6, 9) as "the glory of the Lord shall be revealed and all flesh shall see it together ... Behold the Lord God comes with might, and his arm rules for him" (40:5, 10).

With exceedingly beautiful language Isaiah 41:7-20 portrays the return of the exiles and their passage through the desert as God's new creative act. The argument proceeds with a constant switching between creation, exodus, and promise, and with a systematic correlation of the first things and the new things (42:9).

Chapter 43 continues this by interpreting the election and formation of Israel as a divine act of creation (43:1). Israel's creator is also its saviour (43:3) and once more as in the exodus Yahweh promises that "when you pass through the waters, I will be with you" (43:2). God will give the nations as ransom to carry out the reunion of those created for his glory who had been dispersed (43:7).[14] The one who had made the first things and destroyed Egypt in the Red Sea

---

[13] This paradigm is present, for example, in 40:3; 41:17-20; 42:16; 43:2ff; 43:16-21; 44;27; 48:20ff; 49:10; 51:9ff; 52:11ff; 63:11-14.

[14] Egypt, Cush and Saba were the parts of Africa known by the Israelites. "Ransom" seems to look both back to the death of the firstborn Egyptians and forwards to Cyrus's conquest of these countries.

(43:16ff) will do new things for the people that he has created (43:21ff). He will once again open a way in the desert, make rivers emerge in dry land, and receive honour from the beasts of the field (43:19ff). Among the promised new things is the forgiveness of sins "I am he who blots out your transgressions … and I will not remember your sins" (43:25). Throughout this passage the author underwrites the constant correlation between creation and exodus, both old and new. As the author cannot understand salvation apart from this correlation, we also cannot understand the gospel separate from its roots in creation and exodus.

Isaiah 51:9-16 weaves these same themes together in another message of hope from the perspective of salvation history. After remembering Abraham and Sarah (51:1-2) it returns to the theme of creation promising Zion that God "makes her wilderness like Eden and her desert like the garden of the Lord" (verse 3). This promise will be fulfilled in this world (verse 4ff.) and in the future world when salvation and justice will be fully established (verses 6-9). The prophet then returns to the past to describe the exodus in terms derived from creation, the struggle against Rahab (verses 9ff), which he subsequently links to the return of the exiles (verse11). Israel's comforter is the Creator of the heavens and the earth (verses 12-16). When Israel ceases to drink the cup of God's wrath (verses 17-20), God will hand this cup over to those who have tormented Israel and force them to drink it. Once again, God's activity, from creation until final judgement, is completely interlinked so that each element interprets the others and is interpreted by them. There is one, indivisible history of salvation which starts and ends with God's powerful creational activity.

New Creation and Salvation

When Isaiah describes the return to Canaan and the conditions in the renewed land, he starts to paint an idyllic portrait which in the end exceeds any historical reality. God "makes her wilderness like Eden, her desert like the garden of the Lord" in which salvation and justice will be born (51:3, 6-8). "I will make a way in the wilderness and rivers in the desert. The wild beasts will honour me" (Isaiah 43:19-20). This passage, as with Isaiah's whole creation and exodus framework, seems to initially refer to the return from exile, but at the same time it opens new perspectives that portray "new things" in eschatological proportions. "Moreover, the light of the moon will be as the light of the sun, and the light of the sun will be sevenfold … in the day when the Lord binds up the brokenness of his people" (Isaiah 30:26 see also Ezequiel 34:25; Amos 9:13-15; Micah 4:1-4, Joel 3:18, Hosea 2:18, 21ff).

This cannot be reduced to the delirium of a frustrated exile; it was the first glimpse of the eschatological vision of a new world. Some passages explicitly state that the future glories will follow the culmination of the current world (51:6-8; cf. 24:1-5, 17-23; 34:2-10). Significantly, these passages represent the end of the world as a "de-creation", the unravelling of the work of Genesis 1, step by step, in reverse order. The new which God is announcing will be a new creation superior to God's previous work. The prophet seems to realise that he has gone beyond the parameters of the first things, the already existing realities, and has started to visualise a qualitatively new order not yet imagined. Just as God had announced in anticipation the former things, which were fulfilled, now he is announcing new things which also will be fulfilled.

Gerhard von Rad emphasises the radical nature of this vision: Isaiah, Jeremiah and Ezequiel "combated without interruption all ideas that came from the past, all restorative tendencies and revisionist hopes. These prophets spoke about a new reality that Yahweh was going to create" (1972:120, 164). With this the prophet "spoke against the original creed of Israel, inviting the nation to place all its existence in God's future salvific work" (1973:309, 339, cf. Driver 1991:172-174). For von Rad this vision destroys prior existence with an explosive force and opens the way towards the novelty that God brings.

This prophetic vision reaches its peak in the final chapters of Isaiah. Isaiah 65:16b-25, a masterpiece of prophetic literature, starts with the familiar contrast between the first and the new things. The triumphant announcement of the new creation is surrounded by a foursquare invitation to forget.[15]

> 16b: because the former troubles are forgotten, (1)
> 16c: and are hidden from my eyes. (2)
> 17a: For behold, I create new heavens and a new earth; (announcement of new creation)
> 17b: and the former things shall not be remembered, (3)
> 17c: or come into mind. (4)

Previous messages had also encouraged the disconsolate exiles to leave their obsessive gaze to the past and direct their eyes to the future:

> 42:9 Behold, the former things have come to pass, and new things I now declare.
> 43:18ff: "Remember not the former things, nor consider the things of old.
> Behold, I am doing a new thing.
> 48:6 ff: "You have heard; now see all this; and will you not declare it?
> From this time forth I announce to you new things,
> hidden things that you have not known.
> They are created now, not long ago; before today you have never heard of them,

Jeremiah uses the same language of contrast between the old and the new, in a relative rejection of nothing other than the ark of the covenant: "in those days, declares the Lord, they shall no more say, 'The ark of the covenant of the Lord.' It shall not come to mind or be remembered or missed; it shall not be made again" (3:16; cf. 23:7ff; 16:14ff; 23:7; 31:31ff).

These repeated invitations to *forget* the past surprise us in a prophet such as Isaiah who has such a powerful sense of history and who regularly exhorts the people to remember God's great gestures and *not to forget* the past (44:21;

---

15 This invitation is expressed in future verbs which functioned as exhortations for the reader; they can be compared to the future verbs used as imperatives in the Ten Commandments.

46:8ff). The same prophet portrays the future based on elements of salvation history such as creation, pact, exodus, and exile. The author not only calls the people to hope but assures them that the new will surpass the old to such an extent that there will be no room for nostalgia, which should be left behind. There will be no repeat of what happened with the second temple, when those who could remember the glories of Solomon's temple cried in the face of an unfavourable contrast (Ezra 3:12; Haggai 2:3).

This prophetic mentality definitively marks the messianic and eschatological hope which reaches its fullness in the New Testament. God's salvific action is one and in continuity with creation, covenant, exodus, the return from exile and coming kingdom. Each one is configured by the previous which it reinterprets and presents anew. Each one makes the others present in the new historical situation; none can be understood apart from its relationship with the others within the total coherence of salvation history. The new neither cancels nor contradicts what came before, although in fulfilling what came before the new surpasses it. We need to understand the salvation that we proclaim in these biblical terms. Creation, exodus, covenant, and the kingdom do not lose their meaning in the gospel, on the contrary, they acquire new meaning and strength and need to be decisively present in our proclamation.

The prophet only begins to glimpse God's surprising designs and describes them in theological and symbolic language. Thus, for example, to interpret the reference to death in Isaiah 65:20 and debate whether it refers to the millennium (Revelation 20) or the final state (Revelation 21) is to seriously misunderstand the prophet's thought. For Isaiah "the new is emerging as a green shoot" (von Rad 1973:339). The previous promise "has already arrived" and the new "is on its way" (Isaiah 42:9; 43:19) germinating in Cyrus' victories (Moriarty 1961:272ff; cf. García Cordero 1967:347, 350). To interpret this passage as exclusively referring to the prophet's and our future is to remove it from its context thus committing exegetical violence.

Curiously, after announcing "the new heavens and new earth" the prophet does not focus on the physical aspects of the new world, but on the human and social elements. (1) There will be joy in creation and in community (65:18ff).[16] (2) There will be life and longevity, as in the days before the flood. To die at a hundred will be to die as a child as if it were a punishment (65:20). These original phrases hyperbolically express that death, in effect, will be defeated. (3) Workers will not be alienated from their labour, neither by war, nor by unexpected death by pestilence, nor through economic exploitation. (4) Likewise, systems which "bear children for calamity" (Isaiah 65:23b) will no longer exist. (5) God's blessings to Abraham will be fulfilled (65:23b-24). (6) There will be communion with God (65:24). (7) There will be harmony in all of creation (65:25). Animals, and especially humans, will be vegetarians as before the flood. It is an integral

[16] "Joy", "gladness" and "rejoice" appear repeatedly in these two verses: "But be glad and rejoice forever in that which I create; for behold, I create Jerusalem to be a joy, and her people to be a gladness. I will rejoice in Jerusalem and be glad in my people; no more shall be heard in it the sound of weeping and the cry of distress. (Isaiah 65:18-19).

hope, qualitatively new, stunningly daring! With this dramatic vision, eschatology reaches a new stage and its maximum dimension in the Old Testament.

Raymond Fung describes what he calls "Isaiah's agenda" under four contemporary points: the end of infant mortality, old age with dignity, homes for all and work for all. "The God we believe in protects children, gives power to old people and walks alongside workers" (1992:2). This vision faithfully corresponds to the utopic justice of many biblical passages, especially in the jubilee tradition (see Leviticus 25:8-23; Deuteronomy 6:10-12; 8:7-18; 15:1-8; Luke 4:17-19; Acts 2;42-47; 4:32-37).

The vision of a "new heavens and new earth" clearly points to the complete fulfilment of the Creator's intentions. This fulfilment both introduces novelty and transcends the past. The new creation is in continuity with the past creation that it fulfils so that the future age does not deny creation as a physical reality but transforms and perfects creation. This perspective characterises Hebrew thought in general, and its opposition to the Platonic concept of a spiritual heaven with no earth: the final state is the realisation of life and community, either on this earth or a new earth. For the prophet, the perfect life cannot be conceived without a new community, and this community cannot exist without a new context, a new, real, physical world.

All of the new creation will be organised liturgically, with the rhythms and melodies of worship (Isaiah 66:21-23). It will be a community of worship and joy. People will come from all nations, to bring their offerings and worship the creator; God will also choose priests from among the Gentiles (66:20ff). If the first creation culminated in worship on the seventh day and the exodus with the worship of the redeemed, the new creation will be a continuous liturgy to the creator of justice and joy, when the unjust will be destroyed for ever (66:24).[17]

---

[17] See also Schökel-Sicre 1979:1:395; cf. Zachariah 14:16.

Creation and Salvation in the New Testament

The New Testament introduces significant changes into creation theology: (1) with Christ the "fullness of time" has arrived, and the age to come and the last days have begun (1 John 2:8). For this reason, Christians live in the time of the decisive accomplishment of God's goals for creation and history (Guelley 1979:65). (2) The same Christ that the disciples had known in the flesh, with whom some had lived and walked through the hills and valleys of Palestine, is the Creator of the universe. For this reason, creation needs to be understood Christologically. (3) In his flesh, by his blood, Christ has reconciled the universe with God (Colossians 1:20). The Bible presents the eternal Word, who had become flesh, as the cosmic Christ. (4) Christ is the goal of creation because all things, in heaven and on earth, will be "recapitulated" in him (Ephesians 1:10). Finally, (5) the New Testament expands the understanding of a new creation as the transcendent end of the historical process (Romans 8; Revelation 21-22).

Edward Schillebeeckx, in an extensive study on "creation and grace" aptly focuses on the New Testament's understanding of creation. Schillebeeckx points out that in their mission to the Jews, the apostles assume the theme of creation almost without mentioning it. Nonetheless, among the Gentiles they followed the Jewish model of missionary proclamation (1977:515-530). Jewish proselytism among Gentiles taught that the only true God[18] was the Creator. The Jewish model was based on a tripart creed: (1) faith in the only Creator God; (2) judgement for those who do not repent and (3) eschatological hope for the converted. These three points can be found in Paul's evangelistic sermon in Athens (Acts 17:22-31). Schillebeeckx indicates that New Testament teaching concerning creation has a hymnodic and liturgical style, as an expression of the Creator's infinite grace.

Pedro Trigo also emphasises the evangelical sense of creation Christology. Trigo affirms that in the New Testament creation cannot be understood separately from salvation, nor can salvation be understood separately from creation. Creation in Christ means that the grace which redeems us has been present since the start of history. For Trigo, in a Christological sense there has never been an age under the ultimate power of sin (1990:33). We can affirm that since creation Christology has cut the roots and relativised the power of evil. Even when we cannot perceive the triumph of grace in the present, it will be

[18] See the theme of the "only God" in the proclamation of the good news in Acts 14:15, 17:22-31, 1 Thessalonians 1:9, 17; cf. Romans 16:27, John 5:44, 17:3, Jude 4, 25).

manifest in the final unravelling of history. Trigo thus analyses, in the light of creation, the great New Testament themes of the cross, resurrection, ascension and the parousia (1990:11-48; cf., Ruiz de la Peña 1986: 76).

New Testament creation theology offers us abundant theological riches. We are only able to analyse some of the most important passages, which are representative of the thought of the main New Testament writers.[19]

John 1:1-18: Creation and Incarnation

It is noteworthy that two of the four gospels start their account evoking the *bereshith* of Genesis 1:1. "In the beginning" (John 1:1) and "The beginning of the gospel of Jesus Christ" (Mark 1:1). Many interpreters have concluded from this phrase that the authors deliberately focused on the gospel as a new creation (Ruiz de la Peña 1986:79; Guelley 1979:67). In both cases, the highlighted use of "beginning" seems to have a theological force. The connotations of this word can be compared to the suggestive power of the number twelve when Jesus, by "creating" exactly twelve apostles (Mark 3:14 *epoisen*) conveyed clearly that he was founding a new Israel (Driver 1991:174). In John's case, the reference to creation becomes explicit in the subsequent passage, with its impressive creation Christology (1:1-3, 10).

Why does John, inspired by the Holy Spirit, insist on immediately introducing the theme of creation? Would it not be sufficient to affirm Christ's eternal deity and move on directly to the themes of incarnation and redemptive death? Creation is inseparably related to the full argument of the prologue, not just the incarnation, as the *sarx* is created matter, but to the new creation through new birth (1:12ff), revelation (1:14, 18) and salvation (1:9-12, 16ff). For John, as for Isaiah, the gospel needs to be understood in correlation with the creation of the world and God's purpose for the whole universe.

There has been much discussion concerning where John derived the title *logos,* word, and how he understood it. John usually is influenced by the Old Testament. In Genesis 1, God made everything in the beginning through his speech (cf. Psalm 33:6) so that in John 1 the Word has created the universe (1:3ff, 10, *tá pánta).* Alternatively, Proverbs 8:22-31 affirms that wisdom was with God in creation, with a similar role to that of the Word in John 1:1-5. In wider terms, the prologue is faithful to the prophetic realism of the Old Testament and its affirmation of the physical world as God's good creation (see Bowman 1955).

It is also probable that John, writing in Asia Minor where many philosophical ideas circulated, also thought of the *logos* concept present in various Hellenistic philosophical schools, such as Stoicism, Platonism, and subsequent Neoplatonism. Adolf Harnack (1892) and others have suggested that John's prologue is more than an introduction or summary of his gospel, but a means of

[19] Driver offers us a deep exposition of the same passages we will look at (1991:171-186). I only discovered this valuable book when I had finished my own manuscript and I was pleasantly surprised that working independently, our biblical study has led to similar conclusions.

preparing Hellenistic readers to read the gospel by employing relevant language and concepts. The prologue thus handles an intentional ambiguity, being comprehensible for Hebrew and Hellenistic readers in their respective semantic registers.

In Hellenistic philosophy, the *logos'* basic role was to separate God from material creation, which was seen as bad and unworthy. Gnostic schemes subsequently elaborated this through numerous pairings of semidivine couplings, from the *logos* and *sophia* which were closer to God, "with God" (John 1:1), to the significantly inferior *demiurge,* guilty of creating matter.

Philosophical teaching which completely rejected creation and matter was present in Asia Minor, so John strategically starts his gospel with language much appreciated by philosophers: the *logos* who was with God and was God, was in the beginning with God (1:1). Any idealist philosopher would be content with such a declaration. However, in what follows, John deals two mortal blows to this pagan rejection of physical creation: (1) it was this *logos* and not the despised demiurge who created all things without exception, including matter; (2) furthermore, this *logos* went to the extreme of becoming flesh (1:14). Against the rejection of matter by pagan metaphysical idealism, John once again reaffirms the goodness of creation in Genesis 1 in all its materiality.

The relationship between creation (1:3ff) and flesh (1:14) demonstrates that creation is essential to the gospel. Jesus' physical humanity, his *sarx*, mediates God's maximum revelation (cf. Acts 1:1-3) and salvation. Curiously, the previous verse employs *sarx* in its negative sense, we are not born "of the will of the flesh," and the next use of the term will also be unfavourable 3:6 "That which is born of the flesh is flesh." In these passages the meaning is obviously ethical rather than physical.[20] The only other Johannine reference to *sarx,* the lengthy passage in 6:51-56, Jesus' flesh, his physical body, is described as the bread of heaven which gives life. In 1 John 4:2ff and 2 John 7, the spirit of the antichrist is identified by specifically denying that Jesus came in the flesh. All this is a definite denial of the Greek dualism between flesh and spirit and the corresponding rejection of material reality.

Peter and Paul also emphasise the decisive importance of Christ's physical flesh in his salvific work. Romans 8:3-4 is particularly interesting: "For God has done what the law, weakened by the flesh, could not do. By sending his own Son in the likeness of sinful flesh and for sin, he condemned sin in the flesh." The first use of flesh is in a negative, ethical sense, the second is in a literal material sense. This word play between flesh in a negative ethical sense and a physical salvific sense, is present throughout Romans 7:5-8:12. In Ephesians 2:14-15, Paul declares that Christ has reconciled us and "has broken down in his flesh the dividing wall of hostility ... that he might create in himself one new man." Likewise, in Colossians 1:22 we read that Christ "has now reconciled in his body of flesh by his death." Peter similarly declares that "Christ also suffered once for

---

20 Likewise, in 8:15 "you judge according to the flesh." 1 John 2:16 presents a similar polysemy in John's use of "world".

sins ... being put to death in the flesh but made alive in the spirit" (3:18) and that "Christ suffered in the flesh" (4:1). John, Peter, and Paul are not ashamed of the physical sense of Christ's flesh but see it as central and indispensable for salvation, and repeatedly insist that our redemption comes about through the *sarx* of the incarnate Word. Without this flesh there would be no salvation.

The argument in John's prologue, confirmed by the "fleshly soteriology" of Paul and Peter, clearly reveals that God's strategy for our redemption was not to annul nature and rescue us from all that is material and physical, but to personally enter, in the most profound way imaginable, this physical and material reality. The Creator redeemed his creation by becoming a creature, a physical part of his own creation, to inaugurate with his life, death, and resurrection the new creation promised by the ancient prophets.

Colossians 1:15-23

This Christological hymn correlates, with a close parallelism, Christ's role as mediator in creation (1:15-17), and in reconciliation (1:18-20). Once again, this structure reveals the theological relationship between creation and salvation. The redeemer is the "firstborn of creation;" the Hebrew equivalent, *becoro shel olam,* was a rabbinical title for Yahweh and the Messiah (Lightfoot 1886:145). According to Colossians 1:16-17:

> For by him all things[21] were created, in heaven and on earth, visible and invisible,[22] whether thrones or dominions or rulers or authorities—all things were created through him and for him.[23] And he is before all things, and in him all things hold together.[24]

Colossians 1 and the parallel texts we have referenced reveal the continuous link between creation, salvation, and the mission of the church (1:23). For Paul, or the pre-Pauline poet who probably composed this hymn, it was necessary to introduce this vast creation Christology. Christ's role as the one who creates and sustains the universe is the basis to understand his work of reconciliation. What the Son did in creation, he continues in salvation; what he does in salvation is essentially a renewal of what he did and does in creation.

There is a structural parallelism between the second half of the hymn, on Christ as the mediator of reconciliation, and the first part with the same expressions being used in both stanzas. The "firstborn of all creation" (1:15) is also "the firstborn from the dead" (1:18). "In him all things were created" and "in him all the fullness of God was pleased to dwell" (1:16a and 1:19). "All things were created through him and for him" in heaven and on earth (1:16) and through him all things were reconciled (1:16, 19), in heaven and on earth (1:20).

---

[21] *Tá pánta,* the universe. Cf. John 1:3.

[22] Cf. Revelation 4:11, 5:13.

[23] Cf. Ephesians 1:10, God's design to "recapitulate" *tá pánta* in Jesus Christ.

[24] Cf Hebrews 1:3: "he upholds *tá pánta* by the word of his power".

As Creator he is "before all things" (1:17), as Redeemer he deserves all pre-eminence (1:18). This passage is an example of what TW Manson calls "a parallelism of complete verses" (1931:54-56).

This passage introduces another important novelty in creation Christology. Ruiz de la Peña points out that the formula "for him" (1:16, *eis autón;* cf. 1:20), is applied for the first time to Jesus Christ. Before, as in 1 Corinthians 8:6, Christ is the mediator of creation *(di' autou, en auto)* but has not been assigned as the ultimate cause of the universe *(eis autón)* (1986: 74).

This hymn describes the three eras of creation Christology: all was made through Christ, in the present all exists in Christ, and in the future, all will culminate in Christ. In other worldviews, according to Ruiz de la Peña, the focus is exclusively on the past, only in the Bible does faith in creation transform the future of the universe (1986:85). For this reason, as Jürgen Moltmann reminds us, "faith in the resurrection is the Christian form of faith in creation" (1987: 80).

We also should not ignore a final point. This passage, as the Bible itself, begins and ends with creation. When Jesus spilt his blood on the cross, God not only erased our sins and reconciled us with himself but also reconciled "to himself all things, whether on earth or in heaven, making peace by the blood of his cross" (1:20; cf. Hebrews 9:23). Christ the Creator reconciled the universe (1:20) and brought about reconciliation among us (1:21-23). This cosmic reach of Christ's work of reconciliation can be seen in other passages. Consequently, biblical soteriology, at all times, has its foundation in creation theology.

Romans 8: Creation's Birth Pains

Romans 7:7-8:39 is one of the most surprising and significant texts for our theme. Starting from an intensively personal point of view (7:7), it is a passage with strong contrasts and great surprises. Initially, Paul is pessimistic and defeatist when faced with the power of sin (7:7-24). He starts with one of the saddest paragraphs in all the New Testament and ends with one of the most triumphant expressions of a theology of hope (8:28-39). Paul begins from an agonising existential problem and achieves a theology of creation, history, and hope.

This passage initiates with the tragic history of defeat and despair, possibly Paul's own, in the face of our sinful nature (7:7-24) asking who will deliver us from the "body of death" which weighs upon us (7:24)? Yet when he has reached the pits of despair, the apostle breaks out in praise and gratitude to God because "the law of the Spirit of life has set me free in Christ Jesus from the law of sin and death" (Romans 8:2). There is a lengthy exposition of the ministry of the Holy Spirit in the life of a consecrated Christian (Romans 8:5-16), a classical passage on the victorious life. In 8:17ff Paul recognises that we still suffer afflictions, but these are insignificant when compared to "the glory that is to be revealed to us" (verse 18).

At this point we encounter the most unexpected turnaround in the passage. We would logically expect a reference to heaven as our final dwelling place, "way beyond the blue" to come after the mention of the "glory that is to be revealed." Instead, Paul does not describe heaven but refers to creation (verses 19-23). To our complete surprise, Paul understands "the glory that is to be revealed to us" (verse 18) not as "heaven" but as the new creation. The Holy Spirit's final victory, inaugurated in Christ's resurrection (verses 10-13) and manifest in our Christian life in the Spirit (verses 1-16) will be fully realised only when we rejoice in the glorious freedom of the new creation in our resurrected bodies (verse 23).

Meanwhile, creation groans with birth pains (verse 22) and we in the Spirit and with the Spirit accompany this impatient groaning (verses 23-26). Our hope is firm, as we know that no created thing can separate us from God's love (verses 28-39).

For the apostle, the answer to the problem of personal sin (7:7-24), lies in the full theology of history, creation and freedom developed in chapter 8. He inserts the personal story of defeat and spiritual victory in a historical vision that goes from Adam's sin (8:20) towards new creation and the final resurrection (verses 21-23). Thus, Paul insists that we are not the only ones to be liberated (7:24; 8:2, 15ff) but that "creation itself will be set free from its bondage to corruption and obtain the freedom of the glory of the children of God" (verse 21).[25]

If, like Paul, we groan under the weight of sin (7:7-24), we need to understand that creation itself does so, albeit as the birth pains of a new creation (8:22). Through the Holy Spirit, who also intercedes with unutterable groanings (verse 26), our groans are united with those of all creation as the birth pains of freedom. A new world is about to be born within the womb of the old order. The cry of the earth here is not the agony of the planet Earth but the cry of the birth of a new creation.

The language of birth is part of the vocabulary of creation. The mountains (Psalm 90:2, Job 15:7), the rain, dew, and ice (Job 38:28ff) and human beings (Job 15:7) have been "begotten". At its creation, the sea "burst out from the womb" (Job 38:8, cf. Foerster 1965:1009). Yet the emergence of the new creation is not a painless birth.

In Romans 7:7-8:39, Paul places creation and humanity in a parallelism which corresponds to the Christological parallelism of Colossians 1:15-20, and which also corresponds to the typical correlation between creation and salvation throughout Scripture. In sin (vanity) and in salvation (freedom) we share the same destiny with all of creation. Through the fall, the cosmos has been subject to vanity (8:20; cf. Genesis 3:17) to end up becoming a "giant circle of futility" (Foerster 1965:1031). Human nature is under the same futility (Romans 7:7-24) "weakened by the flesh" (8:3). The covenant of grace is made with humanity and with all of creation (Genesis 8:21ff; 9:8-17), yet human sin continues to grieve the earth (Jeremiah 4:22-26; Hosea 4:1-3), provoking cosmic groaning (8:22).

---

[25] Paul sees this corruption as a consequence of sin, see Romans 8:20 for example. Driver (1991:183, note 41) mentions some authors who defend that *ktisis* here is not a reference to what we consider nature but to humanity. Nonetheless, the links with the biblical theme of new creation suggest a wider sense.

This time of futility and groaning gives way to God's grace and patience. The final redemption will bring full liberty both to the children of God and creation.

The passage appropriately ends full of hope and joy (8:28-39). If our own sin causes defeat and death-in-life, the Spirit not only gives us victory in Christ but also reveals that our salvation belongs to a new narrative of life (8:2, 6, 10ff, 13), justice (8:4; cf. Matthew 6:33) and freedom (cf. Galatians 5). Our micro hope at a personal level is founded on this macro hope of new creation at a cosmic level.

It is easy to overlook this fundamental teaching from Romans 8: both our sin and our salvation have cosmic and collective dimensions which go beyond individual circumstances. The theology of the fall and sin means, in the words of René Padilla, that behind the personal guilt of every human being we also find "a victim of an order which transcends them." Padilla eloquently describes this endemic and systemic sin from a biblical perspective:

> Sin, in the singular, is not the sum of individual human sins. It is, on the contrary, an objective situation which conditions humans and compels them to sin … Sin is not, therefore, merely an individual problem, but a social and cosmic problem … personal sins ... are the echo of a voice that proceeds from … the creation which was "subjected to futility" and which needs to be freed from the "bondage of corruption" (Romans 8:20-21).
>
> There is no true evangelisation without the proclamation of Jesus Christ as Lord of all, as Christ's universal authority relativises all the values of the present … the cosmic Christology of the New Testament is at the heart of true proclamation.
>
> Consequently, the only authentic evangelisation is that which is oriented to the ultimate goal of the "restoration of all things" in Christ Jesus, promised by the prophets and proclaimed by the apostles (Acts 3:21). Any eschatology centred on the future salvation of the soul becomes excessively limited when faced with the secular eschatologies of our times … Now, more than ever, the Christian hope with its wider dimensions must be proclaimed with such conviction and strength that it becomes unnecessary to prove the falseness of any other hope (1986:6ff, 11; cf. Schillebeeckx 1980; 527-530).

This has profound consequences for evangelisation and the church's mission. A merely individualistic theology, with an eschatology exclusively destined for the individual soul, will inevitably produce an evangelisation which is also individualistic. In comparison, a biblical theology will produce an integral evangelisation.

2 Peter 3:1-13: New Creation, a Space for Justice

Popular eschatology in evangelical circles has used this passage, with its dramatic vision of a final holocaust, in ways which are not faithful to its content and message. In fact, this is the only passage in Scripture with the image of *destruction* by fire,[26] although this is a popular image in apocalyptic literature, especially the Sibylline Oracles. The Bible offers over ten different images of the end of the present world, which are impossible to reconcile if read literally. The Book of Revelation never suggests the destruction of this earth through an eschatological holocaust, a concept which is incompatible with the book's message. What we find in Revelation, after the passage on the millennium, is the simple statement that "earth and sky fled away, and no place was found for them" (Revelation 20:11). We have already seen how Romans 8 describes the relationship between the old creation and the new creation as a birth: other passages describe the end of the world as an earthquake (Hebrews 12:25-28) and a worn-out garment (Hebrews 1:11), a scroll being rolled up (Isaiah 34:4, Revelation 6:14) or as the "recapitulation of the universe in Christ" (Ephesians 1:10).

From this set of passages concerning the end of the world, including 2 Peter 3 we can draw a consensus on some key points. (1) Our current world will have an end; present creation is not eternal. (2) The end of the world will be a form of judgement and purification, not evolution. (3) After the end of this present world a new creation will follow. 2 Peter 3 highlights this hope emphatically: after lengthy descriptions of the holocaust, the author provides the most important conclusion: "we are waiting for new heavens and a new earth in which righteousness dwells" (3:13). One cannot preach faithfully from this passage if one does not give this short but central statement its crucial significance as the key to comprehend its message. It is surprising how many preach on this passage without mentioning the "new creation where righteousness dwells" (cf. Matthew 6:33).

Once again, as in all of Scripture, we see together the themes of creation (3:4ff, and the flood in verse 6) salvation, judgement (3:7-12) and new creation (3:13). This passage has a practical rather than speculative application. Verse 12, in the Greek, even teaches that our holiness can hasten "the coming of the day of the Lord".[27]

Revelation 4-5: The Liturgy of Creation

As in the exodus, creation dominates the thought of John of Patmos. In the initial greeting God identifies himself as the "Alpha and the Omega" (1:8). The son of man, who appears amid the candlesticks, is "the first and the last" (1:17) and "the beginning of God's creation" (3:14). The victors are promised that they will eat from the tree of life in God's paradise (2:7).

Throughout the book, natural forces such as thunder, lightning, the sea and rivers, the sun, the moon, and the stars, all have a dramatic role. The powerful angel in chapter 10, who commands John to eat from the sweet and sour booklet

[26] Another possibility is Zephaniah 1:18, other passages refer to purification by fire.
[27] See also Revelation 19:8 where our just actions are the fine linen with which the Lamb weaves the wedding dress of his bride.

of his prophetic mission (10:10ff), swears by the name of the one who created all things (10:10ff). Significantly, the angel bearing the "eternal gospel" calls all to worship "him who made heaven and earth, the sea and the springs of water" (14:7). Once again, the axis of creation, revelation, salvation, history, judgment, and future consummation are coordinated.

The throne vision (chapters 4 and 5) which initiates the main part of the book, is particularly inspiring. This majestic heavenly liturgy is a celebration of God as Creator and sovereign over the earth. Above his throne a rainbow shines (4:3), a clear reminder of God's pact with Noah, with all the earth and every living creature (Genesis 9:8-17). Around the throne we have four of these living creatures: a lion, an ox, a human being, and an eagle (4:7). We can understand them as representing "all that breathes," wild animals, domestic animals, humanity, and the birds. The chapter ends with the twenty-four elders worshiping God because "you created all things, and by your will they existed and were created" (4:11). As in the Old Testament, faith in creation is sung and celebrated. It is obvious that creation also led John to sing while in exile on Patmos. His creation Christology was John's starting and reference point: it was a privileged theme in his prophetic theology. John knew that the Christian communities in Asia Minor needed a vision of God as creator and a theology of creation to face the risks and challenges of their times.

In creation all is harmony and praise (chapter 4), but new and anguishing tensions are introduced in history (5:1-4). John's tears find their answer in the new character who suddenly appears: the lamb who was slain (5:6) and is worthy to open the seals! Tears are transformed into song (5:8-14), and the singing grows in concentric circles of praise. It starts with the united choir of the four living beings and the twenty-four elders (5:8-10), and suddenly increases with billions of angels joining in (5:11-12). The liturgy reaches its peak in the cosmic resonance of "every creature in heaven and on earth and under the earth and in the sea, and all that is in them" (5:13). In this way, the litany returns to the theme of creation and resolves the historical tension: the universal throne is that of God and the Lamb (cf. 2:26; 3:21; 22:1). John thus ties together the biblical threads which correlate creation, history, and salvation.

Revelation 21-22: All Things Made New

With its climatic role in Revelation and the whole canon, this passage is central to correctly interpret the biblical message, the gospel, and the mission of God's people. These two chapters can be summarised through three central themes: new creation (21:1-8), new Jerusalem (21:9-27) and new paradise (22:1-5).

As creation theology plays a vital role throughout all the Bible, it should be no surprise that the same occurs in the final pages. Nonetheless, nineteen centuries of European tradition have led us to think in abstract philosophical categories, rather than concrete, biblical ones. I would be bold enough to suggest that most readers assume *a priori* that at the end of everything material reality will disappear, and God will lead us to heaven, the Gloryland way beyond the blue, where we will be pure, ethereal, spirits, forever freed from bodily and material chains. Many, probably most, still read Revelation convinced of these platonic presuppositions so that they simply assume that "new heaven and new earth" and "new Jerusalem" are nothing more than symbolic descriptions of the heaven where God will take our souls.

It is correct that some biblical passages seem to teach certain elements of this heavenly theology. When we die, Christians will be, temporarily, with the Lord; after the final judgement, we will see God face to face, as he is (1 John 3:2). Nonetheless, these are not the most emphatic elements in biblical thought and are not present at the end of Revelation. Revelation 20-22, in faithfulness to the full biblical tradition, presents us with a new creation that is so realistic and physical that many in the ancient church considered the book materialistic and opposed its inclusion in the canon. It is beyond dispute that the last pages of the Scriptures conclude the biblical message with a theology of the new earth rather than a theology of heaven.

Revelation 21-22 is undoubtedly based on the prior tradition of the new creation, especially Isaiah 65:17-25. Just as the last pages of a mystery novel provide the reader with the hermeneutical key to understand the rest of the book, so we should privilege the new creation tradition as the hermeneutical key to understand biblical faith. Nothing in Revelation 21:1-22:5 allows us to think that it is merely a symbolic description of a spiritual heaven; rather everything indicates that it continues the prophetic realism of Hebrew thought and the biblical message in general.

The language used in 21:1 and 21:4b-5a have verbal parallels with Genesis 1 which are not accidental:

> Then I saw a new heaven and a new earth, for the first heaven and the first earth had passed away, and the sea was no more … for the former things have passed away." And he who was seated on the throne said, "Behold, I am making all things new."

The initial phrase "heaven and earth" inevitably takes us to the first words of Genesis 1:1 and warns us that God's plan ends with a completely revised version of the first creation, which nonetheless continues to be heaven and earth. Other elements from Genesis 1-3 are present: the serpent's defeat (Genesis 3:15; Revelation 20:10, cf. 12:9), the sea (Genesis 1:2; Revelation 21:1), death and pain (Genesis 2:17, 3:3, 17; Revelation 21:4), the precious stones (Genesis 2:12, Revelation 21:11, 19ff), the lights (Genesis 1:16; Revelation 21:23), the river (Genesis 2:10-14; Revelation 22:1) and the tree of life (Genesis 2:9; Revelation 22:2).

Other phrases in these chapters incorporate other elements of salvation history: David's Jerusalem (21:2), Moses' tabernacle (21:3), Israel as the Lord's wife (21:2), the covenant with Abraham (21:3), twelve patriarchs and twelve apostles (21:12-14). It is impossible to conceive of a more beautiful way to tie the different threads of biblical thought in a final, integrated way.

Revelation 21:1ff also echoes Isaiah 65:16ff "new heavens and new earth" (65:17b), the old heavens and earth have passed away (see the forgetfulness formulas of 65:16b-17), and the mention of Jerusalem (65:18ff). Revelation 21:5 "I am making all things new" contains a clear allusion to Isaiah 43:19, from the same section of Isaiah. This underlines the conclusion that we have already reached: both Revelation and the Bible conclude with a conscious and emphatic theology of new creation.

This impression is confirmed again, removing any lingering doubts, as Revelation repeats twice, with the same verbal expression, that John saw the New Jerusalem "*coming down* out of heaven" (21:2, 10). According to traditional Platonic thinking, everything should have ascended at the end of Revelation.[28] Nonetheless, Revelation 21:1-22:5 is faithful to Hebrew thought, and everything comes down to the new earth that God has made.

This verbal expression, "coming down," in 21:2, 10 should be enough to confirm the realism of this passage and exclude any possibility of reading it as a symbolic description of heaven. God's transcendental heaven, never passes away, but the "heavens and earth" of the first creation will pass away (Matthew 24:35, Revelation 21:1) to give way to a "new heaven and a new earth." God himself does not need and has never needed new heavens, so this passage is clearly a reference to a new cosmic order, with its earth and atmospheric heavens.

Revelation 21-22 clearly offers no support to the traditional teaching that in the end God will remove us from earth to take us to a groundless and spaceless heaven. There is always the possibility that other passages may teach this hope, this is a task for biblical exegesis. Nonetheless, Revelation 21-22 says nothing about going to heaven, rather it concludes with the affirmation that God will create a new earth and bring both his holy city and his throne to this new earth (22:3).

It is impressive, and typically biblical, that Revelation concludes with a new beginning rather than an end (Peterson 1988:169). The God who makes all things new (21:5) does not simply terminate his first creation, leaving us landless, but completely and perfectly renews it giving us a new and better world. Humans, including John of Patmos need a land, and the Creator wishes to give him one, as he did in the beginning.

Thus, the Kingdom of God is transhistorical rather than ahistorical or superhistorical. The biblical message reaches its peak in a new, transformed, and redeemed history, beyond our current history. This is not a vertical metaphysical transcendence, in terms of a Platonic ascension, but a horizontal salvific historical transcendence, according to the forward-looking pattern of Hebrew thought.

---

28 Or as someone once joked, the New Jerusalem should descend upwards.

Vertical (Greek) perspective

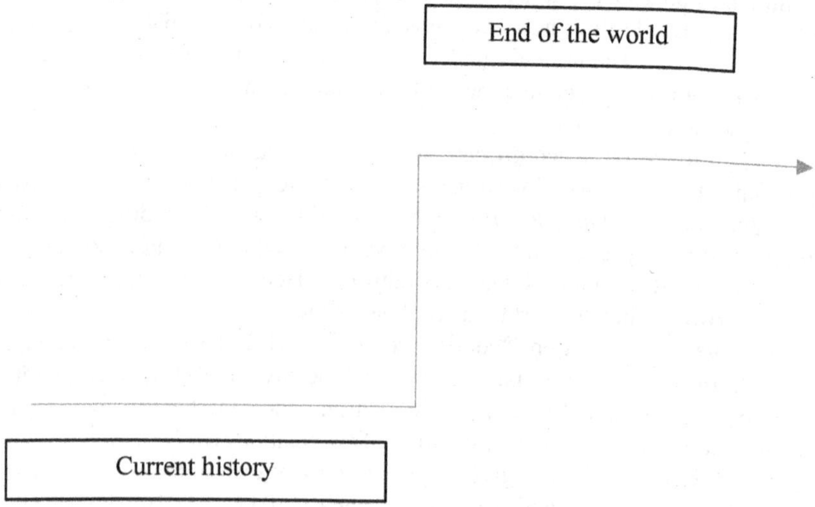

Horizontal (Biblical) perspective

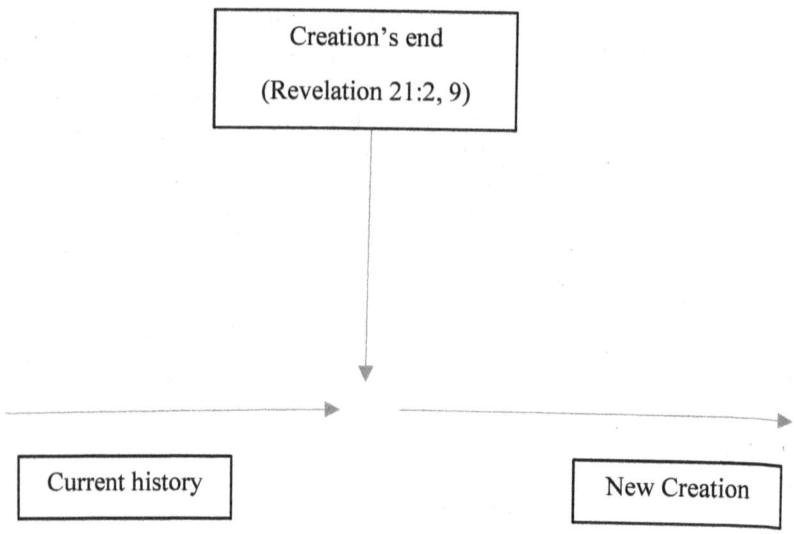

In two lengthy passages, Revelation describes the new creation and its capital city. The first (21:9-21) is an allegorical vision of the New Jerusalem, mainly based on precious stones and symbolic numbers. This set of symbols concisely expresses both the welfare and the abundance of the city with its streets of gold and jewels, and also the links with salvation history such as the patriarchs, the apostles, and the number twelve. Both the verbal expression "come down" and details such as walls and streets indicate that this is not a reference to a heaven above, but to the new creation, announced in 21:1.

There is a sudden change of style in 21:22 towards what can be described as a social analytical description of the new community (21:22-22:5). Once again, this description of life in the New Jerusalem cannot refer to heaven, as the nations walk around the city and the kings bring their wealth (Revelation 21:24-16; cf. Isaiah 2:3, 5, 60:3). This fulfils the numerous prophecies of caravans which would come to Jerusalem (Zechariah 8:20-23; 14:6, Isaiah 61:5ff; 66:12, 20; Psalm 72:10ff) and would be meaningless applied to heavenly dwellings. Furthermore, one of the foundational teachings of biblical eschatology, the resurrection of the body, practically demands a new earth and new city, or community, as the counterpart to a physical, corporeal, resurrected existence and would once more not make sense in a merely spiritual heaven.

Revelation 21-22, like Isaiah 65, focuses on the social aspects of God's promised new order. Rather than explain the physiology of a resurrected body or the meteorology of an ecosystem with rivers but no seas (Revelation 21:1; 22:1ff) Revelation explains to us how people will live together in the new creation. The whole passage can be seen to develop Isaiah 65:18 in its perfect and perpetual fulfilment: "be glad and rejoice forever in what I am creating." We will, therefore, celebrate the feast of the new creation in the New Jerusalem, with the Creator (Isaiah 65:19a, a bridal joy, Revelation 21:2,9). There will be no more weeping or cry of distress (Isaiah 65:19b: Revelation 21:4) and the intuition of Isaiah 65:20, that a child would die at a hundred years, will have become a fulfilled reality as "death will be no more" (Revelation 21:4).

Revelation 21:22 describes how all dichotomy between the secular and the sacred, the temple and the city, is overcome. There is then a description of how the city is illuminated, echoing Genesis 1:16, as God's glory will shine like the sun and the Lamb will be the light which shines in the city (21:23). The seer then describes harmonious international relationships in 21:24-26, as the nations, united together, welcome the Lord. In the new creation, the leaves of the tree of life will bring healing to the nations (22:2). The dragon, who deceives and diseases the nations (12:9; 20:8) can no longer sow war and chaos, while Christ heals and blesses the nations. This new world order includes each nation being consecrated to the Lord with its own idiosyncrasies and particular "glory and honour" (21:26). We can imagine a Paraguayan harp, Nicaraguan poetry, Mexican mariachi and pupusa flatbread from El Salvador. The Greek suggests,[29] in conformity with the already mentioned Old Testament prophecies of eschatological caravans, that not only will people circulate but also cultural and material riches.

---

29 For example, in the use of *timén* in 21:26.

The prophetic tradition's theology of history is what underwrites this socio-political emphasis in Isaiah 65 and Revelation 21. When the prophets spoke about the future, they were always speaking from their own era and to their own era, with strong ethical demands for their readers. Quoting Breneman once more: "it is time that as Christians we become aware of the biblical vision of history, and our responsibility to change and make history" (1984:28).

At the start of his 1974 Lausanne Conference, René Padilla correctly articulated this biblical theme and its meaning for contemporary evangelisation.

> The gospel of Jesus Christ is a personal message: it reveals a God who calls each one of his own by their name. It is also a cosmic message: it reveals a God whose purposes concern the entire world. It is not directed to individuals *per se,* but to humans as members of the old humanity in Adam, marked by sin and death, and called by God to become part of the new humanity in Jesus Christ, marked by justice and eternal life (1986:1).

Some of the responses that I received from the candidates for Clade III (1992) were very eloquent in this respect: "In proclaiming the gospel, we should call individuals not only to be recipients of God's gift but also ambassadors and active workers for the reconciliation of all things in Christ, seeking that society, the environment and the whole universe recover their peace with God." This brother went on to reflect on specific themes such as sexuality, politics, and sport. Another affirmed that creation theology implied, "A new valuing of secular vocations alongside productive idleness, zeal for ecology and the wise use of natural resources, and participation in our history and our world for a more just society which worships the true God." Other respondents affirmed that our evangelisation… "should move beyond an invitation focused on the individual who remains passive until his future redemption, towards an invitation in which he becomes a minister of reconciliation with Christ" and that true evangelisation… "invites us not to escape from society but struggle for its welfare."

From the offset, evangelisation should teach future disciples of Christ that to follow the Lord Jesus means to become resident on earth and incarnate as he first did. It means to take the cross and follow him to the places of great need and pain which surround us. To evangelise and be a Christian means to become a friend of tax collectors and sinners as Jesus did, the greatest friend of the rejected and despised. It means becoming present alongside the victims of war and oppression, alcoholics, drug addicts, the abandoned children of our cities. This is the integral evangelisation which our Lord teaches us in all his Word, the evangelisation that is born of the good news of creation and salvation in Jesus Christ.

Creation and Integral Mission

Our survey of the extensive trajectory of creation theology within the Bible, justifies the conclusion that creation theology is an indispensable key to faithfully understanding the biblical message, and therefore salvation and the church's mission.

Biblical creation theology raises challenging and disturbing questions to our missiology. Does creation theology have the same importance in our proclamation as it does in the Bible? What is the significance for the gospel that the good news reaches its peak precisely in the "new heavens and new earth"? How does the profound statement of evangelical faith in Colossians 1:20, that Christ has reconciled all things on earth and in the heavens fit our traditional proclamation of salvation? How can our contemporary evangelisation be faithful to the message of the new creation? In the face of the avalanche of questions this theme provokes we wish only to comment on some aspects relevant to the church's integral mission.

Salvation History and Integral Mission

One of the most noteworthy features of the Bible is its clear historical nature, narrating, from Genesis to Revelation, the history of how the God of grace acts in salvation (Stam 1992:19-43; Losada y de Angulo 1992). As we have already seen, the Bible presents creation as the start of salvation history. The development of creation theology accompanies the narrative of God's people. This is a long journey which reaches its destination in the proclamation of the new creation, a full confession of faith in the Creator-Redeemer. Furthermore, we have seen that, from Genesis to Revelation, the biblical message is marked by the exodus paradigm and to a lesser extent, by the covenants with Abraham and David, the blessing of the nations, Jerusalem, and the promised kingdom. Thus, when Isaiah prophesies, through the Holy Spirit, the future salvation, he does it in terms of salvation history, such as a new act of creation, a new exodus, a new covenant, etc.

Clearly, the heart of the gospel will always be Jesus Christ's life, death, and resurrection and the first reference of the Gospel, at a personal level, is the announcement of the forgiveness of sins through faith in Christ. Although undoubtedly important, this biblical truth can only be understood in the context of salvation history, "according to the Scriptures" as Paul would say (1 Corinthians 15:3ff).

We need to return to the biblical understanding of salvation history to renew our missiological vision and evangelisation. This involves understanding how God worked for the salvation of his people throughout the centuries covered by biblical revelation. The proclamation of an ahistorical and merely individualistic salvation is not only an impoverishment of the salvation message found in God's word, but also a misunderstanding that leads us, unconsciously, to be unfaithful to the Scriptures and the gospel.

Incarnation and Integral Mission

The incarnation of the Son of God is the definitive mediation of the gospel, therefore the only way to faithfully proclaim the gospel is to proclaim in word and deed an incarnate gospel. There is an obvious contradiction when the incarnation remains simply an abstract idea in our theology and is not lived out in practice. No abstract, ahistorical and antimaterial gospel can be that of the New Testament.[30]

When we analyse how the incarnation paradigm *functions* in contemporary evangelicalism, we observe that it has taken on a secondary role. Some even try to adopt an ingenious argument to defend this. They claim that as Paul supposedly gives little or no importance to themes such as the incarnation and the kingdom of God these would only belong to a first phase in Christian faith. They conclude that in Pauline theology and the mission to the Gentiles, the incarnation and the kingdom were relegated to a secondary level or even lost all their importance.

Although this may be a sincere attempt to faithfully comprehend biblical teaching, it also may cover up the presence of an *a priori* ideology which is being imposed on the biblical text. Nonetheless, this argument naively overlooks a fundamental fact: Chronologically, Paul was the first New Testament writer; all the gospels were written after his epistles. Thus, the incarnation and the kingdom, undoubtedly present before Paul wrote his epistles, continue to be important after the epistles, as they are a central theme in the four gospels, written after Paul's letters. They are, without any doubt, definitive elements in the biblical message and deserve fundamental importance today.

There is an important continuity in the biblical message from the good creation of Genesis 1 until the incarnation and finally the new creation. The Bible always affirms the goodness of physical creation with none of the typical dualisms of Platonic thought. Eugene Peterson has commented eloquently on this:

---

[30] A comprehensive and suggestive exposition of the incarnation is present in Losada and Angulo (1992:159-232).

> We are immersed in materiality from start to finish. At the Genesis beginning we are immersed in materiality; at the Revelation ending we are re-immersed in materiality. Between these boundaries nothing takes place apart from geology and history, geography and weather, incarnation, and sacrament. Our existence is framed in matter. Nothing in the gospel is presented apart from the physical, nor can it be understood or received apart from the physical. That is not to say that there is nothing but matter, for that would deny most of what living by faith asserts. But it does mean that nothing can be experienced apart from matter. The great invisibles, God, and the soul, are incomprehensible apart from the great visibles, heaven and earth (1988:170).

Christ's coming in the flesh means that the Kingdom of God has come, and will come, exactly in the form of flesh and creation. As Karl Barth correctly comments, Jesus Christ came to earth in the power of the new creation (1958:35; 1960:488; 1956:49). Taking on flesh and defeating death in the flesh, Jesus Christ inaugurates the end times, the now and not yet. With the incarnation and the resurrection and at Pentecost (Léon-Dufour 1965:167) the new creation has broken into this present world.

Since Jesus Christ has become incarnate, died and resurrected in the flesh, and his Spirit has dwelt within us, the power of the resurrection also operates in our bodies and lives (Romans 8:10ff, Ephesians 1:19-21). Now we are the first fruits of the coming age, called to be yeast, salt, light and the seeds of his kingdom. Our evangelisation, both in its message and methodology, must be faithful to this biblical reality.

New Birth and Integral Mission

As evangelicals we have correctly stressed the foremost importance of regeneration. The need to be born again (John 3:3-8) and the fact that we have become "new creation" in Christ, by faith (2 Corinthians 5:17) are essential components of the evangelical message, alongside justification by faith, adoption, reconciliation and other biblical aspects of salvation.

Yet, there is an often-forgotten element of regeneration, its direct link with the new creation of Isaiah 65 and Revelation 21. The language of 2 Corinthians 5:17 is easily recognisable in the light of our prior study of Isaiah, Jeremiah 3:16 and Revelation 21-22.

> Is anyone in Christ?
> A new creation!
> The old things have passed away.
> Look! They have become new.[31]

The noun for "creation" (*ktisis)* corresponds to the verbs used in Isaiah and Revelation. Another Greek word, *ktisma,* refers to something that has been created, while the emphasis of *ktisis* is on the act of creating or all of reality as a

31 Personal translation from the Greek. See also Driver (1991:174).

created order (Foerster 1965: 1033-1035). Foerster comments on the use of *ktisis* in 2 Corinthians 5:17 and Galatians 6:15, "the use of the verb *parelthen,* passed away, shows that *ktisis* here is not simply a word for being or human as it is in the rabbis, but carries the full significance of the term" (1965:1034). In other words, it is not just about new individuals but about the eruption of the new creation as the transformed order of all things (cf. Ephesians 2:10, 15; 4:24, Colossians 3:10; James 1:18).[32] As in the first creation, this new creation is by Word and Spirit.

The identical Greek phrase, *kainé ktísis,* is translated as "new creation" in Galatians 6:15 in the corporative sense of Christians as a new humanity beyond the distinction between circumcision and uncircumcision. Thus, the church is the "Israel of God" (Galatians 6:16), created by God as the old humanity in Adam and the old Israel in Abraham. As John Driver indicates, "the church is the community of the new creation in which this restoration has begun through God's grace and the power of the Holy Spirit ... The church is a new creation and a new humanity" (1991:18, 172).

Even more impressively, the phrases we find in 2 Corinthians 5:17c, "the old things have passed away", and 5:17d, "have become new" - *gégonen kainá* - have the same meaning and use the same terms as their equivalents in Revelation 21:1, 4 and its Old Testament sources. They correspond to the formulas of forgetfulness in Isaiah 43:18ff; 48:6ff; 65:16b-17 and Jeremiah 3:16. Paul is clearly affirming that in our regeneration through faith in Jesus Christ the new creation has begun in us as his body. Our new birth is the "now" of the new creation, which will be fulfilled in the end of time.

When we recognise that 2 Corinthians 5:17 refers to new creation we are able to identify the cosmic dimension of the vocabulary it employs. Therefore, we realise that regeneration cannot be fully understood separately from the creation theology it is based in. New birth is clearly a glorious transformation of the believer's personal life, but it is much more: it is a sign and an anticipation of the new creation that God has inaugurated in Christ and will fully carry out when Christ returns to earth in glory and power. Our regeneration introduces us into the new creation as its first fruits and bearers throughout history.

The central theme of 2 Corinthians 5:17 is that our new creation means a complete change of values and criteria, an axiological revolution in how we see things. Paul confesses that he is totally guided by his love for Christ (5:14) who he once saw, "according to the flesh", as a failure and even a blasphemer. Yet now, as new creation, "according to the Spirit", he no longer looks on anyone with the same eyes he used to see Jesus, but sees them in the light of Christ's love (5:16), as anyone who is in Christ is new creation. Therefore, having been reconciled by God's grace in Christ, we are ambassadors of this reconciliation in Christ's name (5:18-20).

The Christological basis for this surprising reality is Jesus Christ's salvific-historical role as the Second Adam (Romans 5:12-21; 1 Corinthians 15:22, 45).

---

[32] Driver's lengthy exposition (1991:174) is very illuminating.

As always, the new thing that God does (Christ) is born from what God has already done in history (Adam). As Christ is the new Adam, and we are united to him, in faith through the Spirit, so we also are new creation.

> Do not lie to one another, seeing that you have stripped off the old self with its practices and have clothed yourselves with the new self, which is being renewed in knowledge *according to the image of its creator.* In that renewal there is no longer Greek and Jew, circumcised and uncircumcised, barbarian, Scythian, slave and free; but Christ is all and in all. (Colossians 3:9-11)

> You were taught to put away your former way of life ... clothe yourselves with the new self, *created according to the likeness of God in true righteousness and holiness.* So then, putting away falsehood, let all of us speak the truth to our neighbours, for we are members of one another. (Ephesians 4:22, 24-25)

The correlation between the first creation, Adam created in God's image, and the new creation, regeneration in Christ, is clear. As in 2 Corinthians 5:16 this is a transformation of values and behaviour. As in Galatians 6:15 what is described is the new humanity in Christ,[33] which overcomes differences between circumcision and uncircumcision, and all discrimination based on race, sex and socioeconomical conditions (Galatians 3:28; Colossians 3:11).

Romans 6:4-6 interprets baptism as a new creation: by the power of the resurrection, we have been born into a qualitatively new life, *kainóteti zoes.* This allows us to understand why James affirms that God "gave us birth by the word of truth, so that we would become a kind of first fruits of his creatures" (James 1:18: *aparchén ton autou ktismatón).* This passage relates new birth, "gave us birth", to the new creation with terms derived from creation, by his word, as in Genesis 1:1. We cannot be the first fruits of the first creation, in Adam, but only of the new creation, in Christ. "First fruits" has an eschatological meaning in James 1:18 and is fully appropriate. By the resurrection Jesus Christ is the first fruits of all those who sleep (1 Corinthians 15:20, 23); the Holy Spirit is the first fruits of the age to come and our resurrection (Romans 8:23); and we are the first fruits of the new creation by the new birth. Paulo Deiros affirms that "the work of regeneration ... is the anticipation of what He proposes to do with all he has created (Revelation 21:1-8)" (1992:98).

When Jesus talks with Nicodemus about the new birth, he explains it in terms of another aspect of the new creation: the Kingdom of God (John 3:3-6). The one who is born again is a new person, whose sins and addictions have already passed in Christ, but also someone who can perceive the Kingdom of God (3:3). To be born again is to enter the Kingdom (3:5). The message of new birth, especially among those evangelicals who describe themselves as born again, must be based on both creation and Kingdom theology. To interpret the new birth apart from the Kingdom, is to impoverish its meaning and suppress an essential element of its biblical formulation. In the language of the parables, when we are born again

---

33 In Hebrew *adam* means humanity so that a new Adam means a new humanity.

between the ascension and the Parousia, we begin to be the yeast, seed, salt, and light of the Kingdom which has come and will come, and the first fruits in the present of the new creation.

When we evangelise, we call and invite women and men to be born again through faith in Christ. Biblically, this means integral mission: challenging people to become disciples of the Lord of the universe, of history, of society and of all dimensions of human life.

Biblical Eschatology and Integral Mission

Every missiology corresponds to an underlying eschatology, as it does to an implicit Christology. Once we understand someone's eschatology, we can tell how they will understand the mission of the church. Our understanding of the final goal of salvation history will shape our understanding of the gospel and evangelisation. Thus, the biblical teaching concerning new creation is essential for the church's integral mission.

Four key themes dominate the Bible's vision concerning the future: (1) Christ's return to earth to reign in glory and power; (2) the resurrection of the body; (3) the final judgment and (4) the end of the world and new creation. These are clearly emphasised throughout Scripture, which correspond to an integral and incarnate evangelisation. Yet contemporary popular eschatology is dominated by secondary themes, often not clearly taught in Scripture: the rapture, the great tribulation, Armageddon, Gog and Magog, and speculations concerning the mark of the beast. This pseudo-apocalyptic focus results in an evangelisation far removed from that which God's word teaches, without its promoters even realising the error of their ways.

This fatal eschatological detour is due to a defective creation theology in which, unconsciously, Greek philosophy trumps a faithful exegetical interpretation of the biblical text. Thus, prophetic doctrines, choruses and evangelistic sermons lack the balance we see in biblical teaching and introduce extrabiblical and clearly antibiblical elements. We see this in the contrast between popular choruses such as "my soul will fly away at the sound of the trumpet, my soul will fly away," and the emphasis on the resurrection of the body in 1 Thessalonians 4:16ff. The flight of the soul is so close to Plato and so far from Paul! The same is true of the romantic vision of the "island of my dreams" and those sermons which invite people to believe in Christ to escape from the great tribulation through the rapture.

In practical terms, many evangelical churches are in danger of reducing Christian eschatological hope to waiting for the rapture. The hope of many Christians no longer seems to lie in the resurrection of the body, the Kingdom of God, and the new creation, but in solely hoping to escape from this world before the great tribulation begins. However, Christian hope lies in our personal meeting with Jesus at his coming, "the one we love without ever having seen." In whatever way one understands the rapture, it should never be more than a secondary detail of "the blessed hope and the manifestation of the glory of our great God and Saviour, Jesus Christ" (Titus 2:13).

It is a terrible flaw to displace the personal and biblical hope of an encounter with Christ himself with the abstract expectation of a rapture which lacks exegetical support. It is extremely serious that our hope lies more in our departure than in his coming. It is extremely serious that people are led into a hopelessness centred on the rapture, rather than a hope centred on Christ, forgetting that he will come to establish his kingdom and judge the living and the dead.

It is important to emphasise that the problem lies not in Pauline teaching, which when correctly exegeted makes valuable contributions to our eschatology. In 1 Thessalonians 4, the apostle is comforting those who cannot understand the death of many Christians before Christ's second coming. Paul affirms that those who have died in Christ will have precedence, they will resurrect first and then we will be taken together to meet Christ. The passage needs to be interpreted in the light of this context: the pastoral problem lies in the death of believers and their fate at the Parousia. This passage has no relationship to the great tribulation or to the presence or absence of the church during the reign of the Antichrist.

The problem is that a vast, speculative, theory had been developed concerning what is known as the rapture with dubious biblical foundations. We believe that the first mistake is the transformation of the Pauline verb "*arpagesómetha*" (1 Thessalonians 4:17) into the unfortunate noun "rapture" influenced by the Latin translation. Secondly, according to the Greek text, Christians, from all times will be taken to meet (*apantesin)* the Lord. Paul is using here the technical terminology used for the Parousia of an emperor and conqueror, when his supporters would come out to meet him (*apántesis)* so that they could enter the city together in a triumphal procession.[34] Nothing in this text suggests that after meeting Christ we are going to spend seven years in heaven.

It is time to return to biblical eschatology instead of the fictional eschatology which dominates our choruses, sermons, and bookstores. The rediscovery of the fullness and richness of biblical eschatology would marvellously nurture a new vision of the integral mission of God's people.

The relationship between realised eschatology, the "now" of the Kingdom which came with Christ, and future eschatology, the "not yet" of the fullness of the Kingdom which will come with Christ's return, is of foremost importance for missiology. The constant tension between the "now" and the "not yet" is a fundamental aspect for understanding New Testament eschatology. As Christ will come to judge the living and the dead, the "not yet", we invite all to repent and receive the forgiveness of sins. As the Kingdom has been initiated and anticipated, the "now", we call all to be disciples of the sovereign Lord (Matthew 28:16-20), and to be light, salt, seed, and the yeast of the Kingdom in their historical and social contexts. The often forgotten "now" of the Kingdom gives

[34] See the analysis of this verse in Bruce (1977) and other exegetical commentaries.

present validity to the message of the Gospel and allows neither an escapist nor a merely futurist evangelisation.

In the previous chapter we referred to René Padilla's arguments concerning the relationship between eschatology and mission. In his speech at Lausanne Padilla declared that "the only authentic evangelisation is that one which is oriented towards the reconciliation of all things in Christ Jesus... The eschatology centred exclusively on the future salvation of the soul is excessively limited", not only in light of the "secular eschatologies of our age", but also of the richness and scope of the biblical vision of history and the future (1986:3).

Padilla develops this perspective throughout his speech. To quote just one paragraph:

> To evangelise is not, therefore, to offer an experience of deliverance from feelings of guilt, as if Christ were a great psychiatrist and the experience of salvation could be divorced from his lordship. To evangelise is to proclaim Jesus Christ as Lord and Saviour, and that through his work humans are freed both from guilt and the power of sin, and integrated in God's purpose to place all things under Christ's command ... The Christ proclaimed in the gospel is the Lord of all, in whom God has definitively acted in history to form a new humanity (1986:10).[35]

Biblical Inspiration and Integral Mission

Paul has left us with the classical definition of the gospel in 1 Corinthians 15:3ff. Nonetheless, hidden within this passage we encounter on two occasions the expression "according to the Scriptures". Paul and Jesus' other disciples were Jews and therefore their mindset was saturated by the Old Testament message as salvation history, and the history of their own people, Israel. "According to the Scriptures" does not merely refer to a handful of proof texts but to the interpretation of all the Old Testament Scriptures in the light of all that God has done since the creation of the world.

Every new stage in the life of Israel was interpreted according to salvation history: creation, covenant, exodus, kingdom. The Jewish prophets projected their prophecies of future salvation according to these themes from the past, especially exodus and creation. The New Testament maintains this historic-salvific hermeneutic. Methodologically, it is evident that "according to the Scriptures" our salvation cannot be understood separated from these main axes of the biblical message.

Specifically, we have seen that the theme of creation/new creation plays a surprisingly noteworthy role in the biblical teaching on salvation, from Genesis to Revelation. Is it possible that such an extensive and emphatic scriptural theme has become excluded from our contemporary understanding of the gospel and evangelistic action? Can we affirm that this biblical theology of creation is present in our current theology of salvation and the mission of the church? Is it

[35] Padilla quotes Walter Künneth to show the relationship between this individualistic Christology and the denial of creation.

not therefore important to face the challenge of recovering this important biblical element in our soteriology and missiology?

It is because we are fully convinced of the inspiration of Scripture that we believe that we must rigorously question all our traditions and adjust them constantly to the biblical message. As we believe in biblical inspiration, we resist adapting the biblical message to anything which distorts its meaning.

The 16th century reformers left us two statements of permanent value and special urgency for our contemporary evangelicalism: *sola scriptura,* Scripture alone, and *tota scriptura,* all of Scripture. *Sola scriptura* means that biblical and exegetical faithfulness requires purging a whole complex of pagan, nonbiblical, dualist concepts from our mentality. *Tota Scriptura* means that evangelical theology needs to be permanently ready to rediscover Christian truths which have been forgotten in time and rediscover aspects and dimensions of the biblical message which have been left in limbo through collective forgetfulness. In the past, the reformers had to amputate many antibiblical traditions which had proliferated for centuries and rescue evangelical truths which had been buried in forgetfulness. We now need to do the same with our own evangelical traditions.

Sola scriptura means that as evangelicals, deeply convinced of the inspiration of Scripture, we must be the first to question our inherited beliefs "to see whether these things are so" (Acts 17:11). *Tota scriptura* means that we should develop our message and mission according to the "full counsel of God" (Acts 20:20). With biblical and evangelical bravery, we should be the first to commit ourselves to the integral mission of God's people according to the good news of creation.

Creation and Contemporary Problems

Creation theology provides a fundamental contribution not only to the integral mission of the church but also to Christian ethics and our presence in the contemporary world. Furthermore, I believe that a clear understanding of creation is foundational and essential for a truly evangelical ethics. This includes micro-ethics, the personal and individual dimension, and also applies to macro-ethics, related to social, political, and environmental issues. In this chapter we will reflect on four urgent themes in our current context of an apparent new world order emerging after the end of the Cold War between North American capitalism and Soviet communism.

Creation and Human Dignity

We have seen that in salvation God restores us "to the image and likeness of the one who created us." Our salvation is, in a biblical sense, a true humanisation, just as sin is always a dehumanisation. Sin spoils and disfigures the image of God in us; salvation restores our authentic humanity.

Fearing secular humanism, some evangelicals have mistakenly rejected the biblical vision of our authentic humanisation in Christ. God's purpose is that we become fully *human.* We should recall the insistence of J. Gresham Machen, a renown evangelical theologian among the first generation of fundamentalists, concerning evangelical humanism:

> after sin has been removed by the grace of God, the Christian can proceed to develop joyously every faculty that God has given him. Such is the higher Christian humanism - a humanism founded not upon human pride but upon divine grace (1946:66).

Biblical teaching concerning the image of God means that our evangelisation should give people back their full dignity as human beings along with the forgiveness of sins and eternal life. Through conversion, those whom society despises learn to walk with their heads high and the poor start to discover the richness of their own value as humans. When evangelisation fosters a faithful biblical theology of ethnicity and culture it allows all to cultivate their full cultural authenticity: as Mayas or Quechuas, as blacks in racist circumstances, as women in our chauvinistic context. Converted to Christ, they will have transformed attitudes towards being black, indigenous or a woman. They will have been reborn to the human vocation of living fully in their own specific particularity. The greatness of their own being as a person will display the beauty and glory of being in the image of God.

Conversion humanises the powerful and privileged with genuine humility and tenderness. It will teach them to deeply respect each human being as the image and likeness of God. Converted they will realise that "those who mock the poor insult their Maker" (Proverbs 17:5; cf. James 3:9). They will recognise that God has made us from just one blood (Acts 17:26; cf. Job 31:13-15; Malachi 2:10) and that the gospel does not allow for discrimination based on race, culture, sex, socioeconomical status or any other reason (Galatians 3:28; Colossians 3:11; Acts 2:17ff). Christians who continue with racial, social, or sexist prejudices have yet to finish their conversion to the integral gospel. We can only imagine the reconciliatory and transformative power that a true integral evangelisation based on a creation theology could have in our divided societies!

If there is no room for discrimination in the first creation, there is even less room in the new creation. Christ, the second Adam, is the pioneer founder of a new humanity, renewed in the image and likeness of its Creator in a way which goes beyond what the old covenant prophets could imagine. In this new creation "there is no longer Jew or Greek, there is no longer slave or free, there is no longer male and female," but a new humanity without discrimination, "for all of you are one in Christ Jesus" (Galatians 3:28; Colossians 3:11). Paul here was possibly refuting an ancient Jewish prayer for the Day of Atonement, point by point (i.e. Greeks, slaves, and women):

> Blessed are you, our Lord, our God, and king of the world, who did not make me a gentile. Blessed are you, our Lord, our God, and king of the world, who did not make me a slave. Blessed are you, our Lord, our God, and king of the world, who did not make me a woman (Women say: Who made me according to His will) (de Sola 1877: I:81).

Paul is telling us that such forms of discrimination have ended for ever in the body of Christ.

In the ancient world, as we indicated in the first chapter, the expression "image of God," was only used with regards to kings. Yet, in biblical thought it becomes a title for human beings. Pedro Trigo develops this theme in his excellent reflection on "The image of God, foundation of human dignity":

> This statement was controversial in a cultural environment in which the image of God was exclusively associated with kings. This rigorous democratisation of what it means to be human, where we all come from and how we all represent the divine was truly revolutionary in its day and continues to be in our own. There is also a dimension which clashes with Western anthropology. In the parallelism of the text "male and female" replaces "image of God" which would suggest that both terms are basically equivalent … The conclusion is that personality lies not in the individual, much less the individual male, but the image is realised in the human community, whose model and prototype is established by male and female.

> Our civilisation is individualistic and does not understand that a person is community. It continues to be chauvinistic; it still has not recognised in practice the differential equality of male and female. It is clear that the established world order disregards the dignity of Third World people; and that discrimination and privilege prevail in Latin American institutions which do not recognise the poor as the image of God. For this reason, we are in a sinful situation. In these conditions an awareness of personal dignity is the greatest treasure a poor person can have (1990:46; cf. Driver 1991:13ff).

Creation theology also necessarily raises the question of *human rights*, and the protection of all who suffer when these rights, which were bestowed the Creator, are abused. Given that the image of God is present in every human being, the Bible prohibits murder (Genesis 9:6, which is even after the fall; cf. James 3:9). According to Genesis chapters 4-11, violence and corruption once more unleashed the power of chaos and opened again the floodgates of the waters, which destroyed the world through the flood (Genesis 1:2; cf. Job 38:8-11).

Against Babel's chaotic projects of violence, injustice and arrogant domination, which attack his creation, Yahweh initiates a project of grace and blessing in Abraham and Sarah according to his creative will and intention. The eloquent creation theology found in Ecclesiasticus 34 led Bartholomew de las Casas to open his eyes to the terrible sin of his fellow conquerors and led to the first struggle for human rights on the American continent. Likewise, an authentic evangelisation in the present will empower the defence of human rights for all, as all are the image and likeness of the same creator.

The example of the Lutheran pastor Friedrich von Bodelschwingh, director of the Bethel home for epileptic boys during the Nazi regime in Germany is eloquent. When Adolf Hitler decreed the elimination by euthanasia of all those considered unworthy to continue living (*lebensunwertes Leben)* the Gestapo went to Bethel to take these children considered socially useless. Bodelschwingh met them with a powerful argument, delivered with implacable conviction to the Nazi police officers: "you cannot take any of these children, as each one of them is image and likeness of God." According to the story, the military left ashamed without taking any children.[36]

In Latin America, creation theology must tenaciously and unconditionally oppose all forms of torture and police brutality, which is so common in many countries, and not unheard of in the United States; as can be seen in the case of Rodney King in Los Angeles, in March 1991, and the subsequent absolving of the guilty police officers. This is just one example amongst many. After the Brazilian military coup in 1964 the refined practice of electric torture spread among all South American countries.

With few admirable exceptions, the standard Protestant response to this sin has been a guilty silence, and at times even an apology for the torturers, in the

[36] If my memory is right, I heard this story at a Karl Barth colloquium. On Bodelschwingh see R. Frick (1957:1335-1337).

name of defending Western Christianity from alleged communist threats. Frequently it is the victims who end up being blamed, a common statement is "if the police got them, it is because they must have done something." Yet, as silence means consent, many Protestants have their hands filled with blood due to their complicity in so many atrocities.

A biblical theology of creation will never allow authentic Christians to remain silent when faced with torture and other systematic abuses of human rights. The Talmud declares the inviolability of human persons in the following way: "Therefore was the first man, Adam, created alone, to teach us that whoever destroys a single life, the Bible considers it as if he destroyed an entire world." The end of the passage also provides us with another reason God only created one initial couple "so that no one should say to his fellow, 'My father was greater than yours" (Glatzer 1962:13ff and note 115).

The Episcopal Conference of Puebla (1979), reflecting on the extent of torture and murder in Latin America declares that "any attack on the dignity of a person is an attack on God himself, in whose image they were created. Thus, evangelisation in the present and future in Latin America demands a clear word concerning human dignity."

As the image of God, every human being has the right to hear the message of salvation through faith in Christ, and Christians have the duty to take this message to them. As the image of God, every human being has the right to a life of dignity. Alongside our evangelistic task, Christians have a humanisation task, to struggle for an ever-improving quality of life for all. This should be seen as an unalienable human right based on creation theology. The good news of creation means a profound theology of human work as liberty and creativity, which contributes to critical reflection concerning our economic systems of exploitative, dehumanising, and inhumane labour (see Trigo 1990:33-45; Losada and de Angulo 1992:41-43: and much of the literature on theology of work).

A true evangelical will always come out in defence of human beings, with significant consequences in diverse situations. It will define the Christian attitude towards extreme poverty which continuously disfigures human dignity and reaps the lives of many. It will lead us to promote public and preventive health to both save the lives of those who cannot afford the necessary medical attention and ensure the minimum conditions for the mental and physical health essential for full and dignified personal development. It will inspire our struggle against economic systems which lead to malnutrition among the poor, victims of the black horse (Revelation 6:5ff). It will inspire our efforts for a dignified home for each family; our defence of public free schooling to give the poor the same opportunities which privileged children receive, and our rejection of wars, whose main victims are innocent civilians, the poor and young.

Creation theology should lead Christians to question the ethical cynicism of neoliberal economic theories, and the antisocial conditions imposed by international credit agencies. Any economic theory which views humans as economic animals, maximisers of self-interest, whose primary measure is money, goes against the image of God.

Robert Bellah narrates an interview with a representative from the Bush administration's Environmental Protection Agency. The interviewer was emphasising the cost in human lives of certain antienvironmental policies established by the agency to defend the interests of large North American industries. When she commented that "some people consider that the value of human life cannot be calculated," the expert, a follower of the Chicago economic school, replied "we have no scientific data to back this up." The value of human life was not part of his equations. His thesis was that a realistic policy, able to provide the national economy with prosperity, that is for the large companies with political influence, required paying a social price in terms of human health, welfare, and eventually, life. Creation theology requires saying 'no' to such reasoning.[37]

Bellah adds that beyond threatening human life, neoliberal market totalitarianism ruined the North American economy. In the end, according to Bellah "Japan reveals that community provides a stronger base for an effective economy than self-interest." Maybe without realising, Bellah provides us with a biblical comment on economic ethics.

Creation and Environmental Stewardship

The environmental crisis is clearly a deeply theological problem related to creation theology. One of the first environmental conferences, in London, reached a deadlock concerning the ethical foundations for environmental preservation, and had to call the theologian William Temple to provide biblical and theological guidance. In more recent years the United Nations Environmental Conference in Stockholm in 1972 practically failed due to a lack of consensus on the moral values which sustain the respect for our environment (See Ruiz de la Peña 1986:191). The UN Conference on Environment and Development (known as the Global Earth Summit) in Rio in June 1992 faced the same ethical dilemmas.

The ecological crisis with its many aspects such as water and air contamination, exhaustion of natural resources, species extinction, destruction of forests, demographic explosion and nuclear weapons threatens human survival.[38] In 1943 CS Lewis had already warned of the danger of the *abolition*

---

[37] *The Nation*, November 25, 1991 (volume 253, number 18), p. 667, extracted from an article in *New Oxford Review*. Ann Swindler carried out the interview for the book *The Good Society (*Knopf, 1991) which she wrote in collaboration with Robert Bellah. The final document of the Santo Domingo Episcopal Conference (October 1992) also warns about the dangers of neoliberal policies (number 180).

[38] Ruiz de la Peña offers a comprehensive explanation of the different dimensions of the ecological crisis. According to his sources, "global levels of contamination double every fourteen years" (1986:183). The consumption of petrol and natural gas doubles every eleven years (1986:184). He warns us concerning the "foolish pillaging and consumption of global resources" (1986:185). Developed countries account for only 25% of the global population, occupy 40% of the land yet consume about 82% of the world's resources, leaving only 18% for the remaining 75%.

of man [sic]. He affirmed that "human conquest of nature will end with humans being conquered by nature." He warned that the few, in subjugating nature, would also subjugate most of society and future generations. Power is concentrated in increasingly fewer hands as "every new power humans achieve is essentially power *over* other human beings." In the end, Lewis affirms, "the final conquest of man is the abolition of man" (see Ruiz de la Peña 1986:188ff, 195).

Certain biblical texts, especially Genesis 1:26 and 28 have been manipulated to theologically justify the irresponsible exploitation of the natural environment.[39] Nonetheless, one clear message in the creation accounts is that God is the only Creator and Lord of the world. Humans belong to the same created order as the earth and animals, and we cannot be lord and masters of that which we have not created. That God has been willing to share his dominion with us allows us, in his name, to help him administer, care, and fill the world. He has placed us as his royal image in all parts of his territory, making us his authorised representatives to carry out his purposes for creation, but this does not include destruction and harm (see Driver 1991: 13-15; Trigo 1990: 45-47; Von Rad 1982:68-72).

Commenting on the second creation account Meredith Kline affirms that the mission is to take care of the earth (Genesis 2:15), a priestly responsibility to care for God's garden as sacred space (Isaiah 51:3, Ezequiel 28:13; 31:9). The same verb, *shamar,* has a priestly meaning in Nehemiah 13:22 and Zechariah 3:7 and is used in allusion to the cherubim in Genesis 3:24 (1877:78). From this we can deduce that our priestly role as Christians also includes faithful environmental stewardship.

The worldview of the Bible is in direct confrontation with the modern technical and industrial perspective and in important ways coincides with the pre-Columbian indigenous perspective. The Genesis accounts underwrite the deep solidarity that humans share with our earth and with the animal kingdom. We have already seen how, according to Genesis 2:7, Yahweh formed *Adam* from the *adamah* (earth). This Hebrew wordplay teaches, in the words of a Nicaraguan poet, that "we are not birds to live off the air, nor fish to live off the sea, but humans to live off the land."

The brilliant and eccentric Dutch painter, Vincent Van Gogh expressed in many genial ways the intrinsic relationship between humanity and the land which sustains us. In one phase of his development he would only paint people with legs which ended in roots sown in the soil, as if from the knees down we were trees. Our indigenous and peasant peoples would understand Van Gogh's paintings better than many university students, whose soles have not touched Mother Earth for years.

Anthropologists have pointed out that for indigenous people their relationship to the land is inherent to their personal and human identity. A saying from the

---

[39] Lynn White (1967) is the most quoted article to blame the Bible for rationalising environmental abuse.

elders of the Miskito people reflects the beliefs of many other indigenous peoples: "a Miskito without land is a dead Miskito." This cultural difference led to many problems between the Sandinista Front and the Nicaraguan Miskitos when the government tried to move them away from the Coco River, a dangerous war zone. Even though their living conditions in Tasba Pri were in many ways better than what they had left behind, they felt displaced and out of control, so far away from their river. Their own surroundings were an essential part of their being, having to live without their river and their forests led to a deep identity crisis.

According to Genesis 1, God created human beings on the same day as humanity, as part of the same act of divine liturgy. Karl Barth comments that human beings, created by God on the same day as the animals, are invited to eat from the same table as them (1958:208, cf. 180ff). Just like us, animals are made from *adamah* (Genesis 2:19) and each one of them is a "living being", *nefesh hayyah.*[40] In Hebrew thought "living" was applied to all that breathed, which included people, animals, and birds, but not plants or trees. As a consequence of human injustice there is a general judgement on "everything on dry land in whose nostrils was the breath of life" (Genesis 6:22) and the new covenant is likewise made with every living being: birds, animals, and humans (9:9). Part of God's mercy upon Nineveh is for the large numbers of cattle (Jonah 4:11), and, strangely for us, both people and animals are commanded to fast and wear sackcloth (Jonah 3:7ff; see Karl Barth 1958: 181). In his famous painting, *Guernica,* Picasso portrays with intense emotion the pain that human brutality, in the bombing of Guernica by Franco's forces, causes animals.

Many biblical passages reveal that humanity and all of creation share a common destiny (Isaiah 11:6-9; 35:2-20; Romans 8; Revelation 21-22). When we practice violence and injustice the earth grieves and is contaminated (Hosea 4:1-3; Isaiah 24:5) and creation groans (Romans 8:19-22; cf. Ruiz de la Peña 1986: 180ff). The profound ontological identification with earth and animals, which seems quaint and primitive to us when we discover it among native peoples, is indeed something biblical which our urbanised and industrialised Western society has lost.

Alternatively, the Bible teaches that, as "older brothers" in the "democracy of all God's creatures" (Saint Francis of Assisi; see Ruiz de la Peña 1986:177; Boff 1982:58-60) we have a great responsibility for all of creation. As the image of God, we are stewards but not owners of the world (Genesis 1:28ff; Psalm 24:1). In the second creation account Adam names the other creatures (Genesis 2:19ff) and thus God establishes him as a collaborator in the creational world, as God himself also named everything he created (Genesis 1:5, etc.). God commissions Adam to work the earth and care for it and invites him to eat all the fruits from the trees (2:15-16). Nonetheless, Adam is not allowed to eat animals (1:29), and this original vegetarianism remains until the flood (9:2ff). Adam is also not

---

40 The term is applied to Adam (Genesis 2:7), fishes and birds (1:21) and animals (1:24); cf. Revelation 4:6ff.

allowed to chop down trees and the Pentateuch prohibits the irresponsible cutting down of forests (Deuteronomy 20:19).

Our modern mentality is unable to comprehend the thinking that lies behind what seems to be the curious and exotic biblical idea of the "sabbath of the land" (Leviticus 25:2-5; Deuteronomy 15). Yet the Bible strongly stresses the importance of the weekly rest for the land and animals (Exodus 23:12). The sabbath festivals, the sabbatical and jubilee years establish strict and ecologically healthy limits on human environmental exploitation.[41] The same can be found in Revelation 11:18's surprising statement: Christ will come to destroy "those who destroy the earth."

The truth, seen first in the biblical creation narratives and later explained by modern science, is that God has created the universe based on laws we must follow, just like the other commandments he has given us. When we abuse the earth, we degrade ourselves and debase creation (Isaiah 24:3-6; Jeremiah 4:12-26: Hosea 4:1-3). When we believe that we are the sovereign lords of the earth, able to exploit it as we wish, we commit the same sin as in Genesis 3, wishing to become gods, owners of creation rather than its stewards. We end up wishing to place our law above God's law, eating from the fruit of the knowledge of ecological good and evil, and once again we break our relationship both with God and the earth. The lack of respect for the environmental laws established at creation could be called the original ecological sin.

Thus, biblical teaching and the serious ecological threat we face make it impossible to separate genuine evangelisation from creation theology and Christian responsibility for the environment. An authentic conversion to an integral gospel, the good news of creation, should lead, according to the logic and strength of God's word, to a genuine conversion towards our Christian duty of stewardship for the environment.

Creation and Justice

It is no accident that the Bible describes the new creation as "new heavens and a new earth, where righteousness is at home" (2 Peter 3:13).[42] Jerusalem, the city of the great king was an "abode of righteousness and holy hill" (Jeremiah 31:23) and the new Jerusalem will be so in fullness. In the new creation "they shall not hurt or destroy on all my holy mountain" (Isaiah 65:25). According to Isaiah 11:9, "they will not hurt or destroy on all my holy mountain; for the earth will be full of the knowledge of the Lord as the waters cover the sea." To know God is to practice justice, judging the cause of the afflicted and the needy, "Is not this to know me? says the Lord" (Jeremiah 22:15).

---

[41] Ruiz de la Peña (1986:175) comments with regards to Deuteronomy 30:15-20 "this impressive text could easily belong to any contemporary ecological manifest."

[42] See the previous section 2 Peter 3:1-13: new creation, a space for justice.

Creation theology, from the outset in Genesis 1, is a comprehensive answer to the problem of evil.[43] In the first chapter of Genesis creation is good at all levels: no monster or evil animal can threaten the fundamental order. Evils which take place do not correspond to creation itself, they are abuses which come because of sin, of anti-creation, the disorder which contradicts the Creator's good order. In John's prologue, creation Christology means light, life, grace and truth. The definitive answer to evil comes with the final victory of the Lamb. The new creation, infinitively good with no evil present, is the "cosmodicy", which will lead to the eternal disappearance of the "mystery of iniquity."

This biblical creation theology allows the Christian to be realistic concerning sin, but always optimistic concerning the triumph of good and justice. According to Ruiz de la Peña:

> Beginning with Genesis 1 .... the doctrine of creation radiates a powerful breath of trust in reality, which opposes the tragic, fatalistic and agonizing readings so often offered in other worldviews ... with faith in creation, evil can never be the central nucleus of reality, nor can it distort one's vision of the world in a way that marginalises goodness... Biblically, the problem is ultimately clarified through soteriology and eschatology... the *eschaton* will be the theodicy, God's justification, and a "cosmodicy", the justification of the world and of history... the New Testament's basic conviction in which Christ is not only the beginning but also the goal of creation, advances the promise of a definitive and irrevocable victory over evil in all its manifestations: the physical evil of limitation, expiry, pain and death; the ethical evil of sin; the structural evil of social injustice, the lack of solidarity between humans (1986:84).

For this reason, the resigned pessimism of many Latin American Protestants is a strange anomaly, especially of those with a more apocalyptic mindset, concerning the possibility of historical transformation relating to justice prior to Christ's return. It seems that all hope and faith is cast on the "not yet" as if Christ had not already come. This fatalist mentality is not derived from the gospel but from other ideological sources and contradicts the fundamental meaning of the biblical message. René Padilla, who has a deep knowledge of our evangelical context, offers a theologically accurate and prophetically pertinent comment:

> In the light of the universal meaning of Jesus Christ, Christians cannot be pessimistic about the world's final destiny. Amid the comings and goings of history, we know that God has not abdicated his throne and at the right time, all things will come under Christ's command ... the only authentic evangelisation is that which is oriented towards this ultimate goal of the "restoration of all things" in Christ Jesus ... (1986:2ff).

---

43 Cf. Ruiz de la Peña (1986:84; 160-162). In fairness one must recognise that, for some, the problem of evil makes it difficult to believe in a good creation and good creator. Trigo (1990: 14) asks the question, "how do we believe in a God of life in a situation marked by death."

This evangelical utopia,[44] with the biblical vision of history and its goal, does not alienate us from our reality but leads us to become involved in just causes. It turns us into eternal rebels, always rejecting the sinful circumstances which surround us, and which contradict the hope of the Kingdom of God and its justice. The distinguished Catholic theologian, Karl Rahner has expressed this in words which have much to say to Latin American Christians:

> Christians should seek to impress their eschatological hope… on the world's social structures… this means that a Christian cannot merely be "conservative" on the social terrain, as their eschatological hope, on the one hand, makes every concrete state of reality relative. On the other, this hope which makes the present moment relative, should be manifest in social structures. In effect, through the eschatological hope of the novelty that God himself brings, Christians are freed from the powers and dominions of the present age (Romans 8:35-39). This is true not only because in the final analysis these no longer have power over one whilst one patiently tolerates their action, but also because one has a firm foundation when facing them – even to the point of giving up one's life- for creative critique and transformation.[45]

Those of us who seek the Kingdom of God and its righteousness (Matthew 6:33) are called to pray that God's will is made present on earth, in our Latin American lands, as it is in heaven (Matthew 6:10). Until now, no one could describe what happens in our countries as God's will, nor do they resemble heaven. Nonetheless, as a popular song indicates, it is insufficient simply to pray for justice, our whole life needs to support our prayer for justice. *Ora et labora,* praying to God and working with our hands, in Christ's name, for the cause of justice in Latin America (see Perkins 1988).

The biblical doctrine of new birth, a key element in creation theology, is also a message of justice. As we indicated in the last chapter, those of us who have been born again are a sign and an anticipation of the new creation and the "Kingdom of God and its righteousness." Every Christian has been "created according to the likeness of God in true righteousness and holiness" (Ephesians 4:24). The noun *dikaiosúne* used here includes our justification before God, but its meaning and its combination with "holiness," as in Luke 1:75, shows that it inseparably includes ethical justice in our new life in Christ (Schrenk 1965:199, 209ff). In the New Testament there is an inseparable relationship between justification and justice.

1 John makes it clear, with powerful language, that the practice of justice is obligatory evidence of new birth:

---

[44] I am using utopia in the sociological sense of Max Weber, Karl Mannheim and others: a vision of a world which can be different, and which leads to a rejection of the *status quo* and a commitment to historical transformations.

[45] For Karl Rahner (1984:920) "novelty" means the last things. Von Rad (1972:175) refers to the "explosive force" with which the prophetic message destroys all the pieces of Israel's prior existence with Yahweh and opens the way for new attitudes. A truly prophetic contemporary Christianity would be like this.

If you know that he is righteous, you may be sure that everyone who does right has been born of him. (2:29)

What we do know is this: when he is revealed, we will be like him,[46] for we will see him as he is. (3:2)

Little children, let no one deceive you. Everyone who does what is right is righteous, just as he is righteous. Everyone who commits sin is a child of the devil; for the devil has been sinning from the beginning… Those who have been born of God do not sin, because God's seed abides in them; they cannot sin, because they have been born of God. The children of God and the children of the devil are revealed in this way: all who do not do what is right are not from God, nor are those who do not love their brothers and sisters. (3:7-10)

We know that we have passed from death to life because we love one another. Whoever does not love abides in death... We know love by this, that he laid down his life for us - and we ought to lay down our lives for one another... How does God's love abide in anyone who has the world's goods and sees a brother or sister in need and yet refuses help? Little children, let us love, not in word or speech, but in truth and action. (3:14-18: putting love into action means giving our life and goods for our brethren).

These texts certainly do not mean that those who have been born again are automatically agents of justice, as if merely by becoming evangelicals we have a monopoly of justice. Nothing could be further from the author's message and the reality of our churches. The argument in 1 John moves along two axes, which have the clear intention of disturbing those born again who were exceedingly "at ease in Zion" (Amos 6:1):

1) Anyone who does not practice justice is not born from God (3:10), no matter how much they go to church and say "Lord, Lord".

2) Everyone who practices justice is born of God (2:29).

In these verses the author reiterates James' argument and goes beyond him in prophetic radicality: all faith in Christ which does not lead to the practice of justice is pure wordiness, and as the prophets insisted, a serious offense against God and blasphemy against the holy name we seek to worship.

If the new creation is going to be a place of perfect justice, Christians should already be God's instruments to create, here and now, spaces for justice in Latin America. We should be, here and now, the salt and the yeast for justice in the Kingdom of God, fermented and anticipated in our lives until he comes. Nonetheless, as evangelicals we lack the moral authority to speak about justice because we are not living it inside our churches. There are painful examples of unjust relationships between mestizos and natives, blacks and whites,

---

[46] That is, just, see 2:29.

missionaries and nationals, and between some ecclesiastical structures and their workforce.

Creation and Reconciliation

Creation means that God made everything in harmony, and new creation means that God will return all things to a state of perfect harmony. New creation means reconciliation with God through faith in Christ, reconciliation with ourselves, with our neighbour and with creation.[47] It also means reconciliation between nations, ethnicities, and social classes, beautifully prefigured at Pentecost and perfectly realised in the international community in New Jerusalem. Through his death, Christ knocked down walls and turned enemy peoples into friends, he "abolished the law with its commandments and ordinances, that he might create in himself one new humanity in place of the two, thus making peace" (Ephesians 2:15, see Yoder *et al* 1992). There can be no discrimination in the new Adam (Galatians 3:28; Colossians 3:11), nor hatred, war, ideological fanaticism, or chauvinistic patriotism.

Jesus Christ declares the peacemakers blessed and true children of God (Matthew 5:9). The disciples of the Prince of Peace should be artisans of *shalom* and ministers of reconciliation in all dimensions of their life. On the other hand, the frightening figure of the red horse in Revelation symbolises the belligerence which "takes peace from the earth" and leads people to kill one another (6:4). Militarism and arms manufacturing scandalously contradict the meaning of the gospel of reconciliation, and no evangelisation can remain indifferent when faced with them.

Jesus affirms that by one's fruits one will be known, and every model of evangelisation should be judged by its fruits of integral reconciliation. This leads to much reflection, especially after the recently concluded Gulf War, for many reasons. Without wishing to offend anyone, but with deep pain and sorrow, I believe that these tragic events are an invitation for us evangelicals to undergo a deep analysis of our conscience. I want to ask a simple question: what were your feelings when you saw the news concerning the Gulf War? Did you respond to this global tragedy with Jesus' love and compassion, or were you infected by the hatred which surrounded us? Did you have the attitudes of a minster of reconciliation in your community, a true son or daughter of God? How many of us cried, with Christ's compassion, for the thousands of victims in this war?

For now, I only want to reflect on two aspects of the Gulf War. The first is the need to reflect on the systematic manipulation carried out by the media[48] and

[47] On the relationship between creation, the cross, and reconciliation with the universe (Colossians 1:20, 1 Corinthians 5:19) see, especially, E. Schillebeeckx (1977:514-516).

[48] A particularly shameful example was the manipulation of the story of the alleged theft of many incubators from a hospital in Kuwait, which left many children dying on the floor. This story was told in tears by a young lady, and powerfully affected all of America and fed much of the hatred against Iraq and raised support for the war. It was later discovered that this young lady was the Kuwait ambassador's daughter.

especially the way in which the new weapons, which had their debut in the war, were dramatically glorified, covering up a great part of the suffering and death of the victims. Many remained absorbed in an almost hypnotic fascination when faced with the impressive use of technologies of death. In fact, many seemed to be enchanted by this war. Where was the presence and voice of evangelical peacemakers (Matthew 5:9) when faced with the cult of the red horse?[49]

Secondly, why did millions of professed Christians allow themselves to celebrate, with such exuberant joy, the deaths of so many human beings, created in the image and likeness of God? We need to carefully examine the ethical implications of the ecstatic hullabaloo which celebrated the allied victory with a body count of maybe a hundred thousand Easterners in comparison to a hundred and fifty Westerners, many of the latter killed by the "friendly fire" of their own troops.[50]

In the United States there were frenetic parades, as if the country had won the football World Cup. In peaceful Costa Rica, which boasts about not having an army, the media, which never raised questions concerning the moral problems of this war, joined in the joyful victory party. On the streets one could see the inevitable shirts and more than one bus, market and canteen was renamed "Desert Storm." The only thing missing was for a public square to be called "Desert Storm" or for an unfortunate baby to be called "Schwarzkopf" in honour of the victorious general!

This example raises questions concerning certain methods of evangelisation. What kind of evangelisation gives birth to millions of evangelicals who join necrophiliac parades hilariously celebrating a war with dubious justification and a massacre of exaggerated proportions? What kind of evangelisation produces converted Christians who become even more materialistic and belligerent than before, seven times more captive to the demon of consumerism and the red horse?

---

49 Many preachers and televangelists publicly supported the war, sometimes sacralising the conflict, making it a holy war. A typical example was the speech by a well-known North American preacher, televised on July 7th, 1991 "we have just celebrated the 4th of July, and I wish to say to all Desert Storm veterans that we praise God for you, we bless you, we pray for you … and for all those belonging to the police, who are in harm's way, we give thanks to God for you". Four months after the brutal police assault against Rodney King, the preacher indiscriminately legitimized the police with such a blessing!

50 The exaggerated firepower directed against Iraqis, mainly to avoid the political cost of North American victims, was a violation of the principles of just war, let alone Christian ethics. The violent attack against soldiers fleeing along the "corridor of death" at the end of the war "was no combat following the norms of *jus in bello* but a massacre, as those burnt had no means of repelling the attack" (Bethke Elshtain 1992:43). Furthermore, much of the allied bombing was aimed with great precision at non-military infrastructure such as water, electricity, purifying factories, transport and communication. Experts from international agencies estimate that the destruction of this infrastructure could cause 75,000 to 100,000 deaths a year, especially of children, in the years after the war.

All this would have had little relevance to our theme if North American evangelicals had not been one of the main social groups to support this war. For over half a century conservative evangelicals have been dominating the religious situation in North America. They are regarded as the hard, solid base of Republican conservativism, and without their support both Reagan and Bush would have had trouble imposing their belligerent policies. Conservative evangelicals have almost unanimously supported wars in Vietnam, Central America, and the Gulf, that have produced the death of so many human beings for whom Jesus shed his blood. The few evangelicals who raised ethical questions concerning the war and abstained from the celebrations were little more than a few brave voices crying out in the ethical desert of the evangelical subculture, which treated them as deluded and dangerous left-wingers.[51]

In contrast, evangelical Christians in Central America have lived the horrors of war, not from the comfort of our television screens but in the towns and fields of our lands, seeing our own brothers and sisters, sons and daughters die. Although there is much we need to repent for with regards to our mistakes and sins during these tumultuous decades, it would be wrong not to express gratitude to the Lord for the courageous faithfulness of a significant sector of the Central American Protestant community and their constructive contribution towards reconciliation. There is a lengthy list of evangelical martyrs and those who have risked their lives for peace and reconciliation. The role of Christian organisations such as CEPAD and CIEETS in Nicaragua or the Lutheran and Baptist churches in El Salvador, have born witness to an integral gospel and a far more biblical and healthy form of evangelisation than that achieved by the focus on success and prosperity in the United States.

Evangelical leaders in El Salvador played a significant role in the peace accords in the beginning of 1992, and many are now working with all their strength for the reconciliation in their nation. For example, one can point to the Salvadorian Baptist Church's strategy for 1992. The project is called "The ministry of reconciliation" and includes a wide range of crucial elements for a ministry of reconciliation, a true incarnation of an integral gospel of *shalom.*

In June I was in El Salvador with Emmanuel Baptist Church, a community marked by its Christian commitment and martyrs. José Duque and I went to a chapel dedicated to the memory of Monsignor Oscar Arnulfo Romero. Even those who disagree with Monsignor Romero's theology are forced to admit that Romero died because he dedicated all his life to the poor, justice, and reconciliation in his country. Yet not even his assassination, and the massacre of nuns and the political opposition, was able to make evangelicals doubt their fervent support for the militarist policy of the Reagen administration.

We also went to the José Simeón Cañas University in San Salvador where the same soldiers who murdered Romero interrupted the evening rest of six Jesuit

[51] Since the second half of the 1980s, aggressive attacks against pacifists in North and Central America have increased, accusing them of being "foolish tools", communist agents.

theologians and two innocent women and murdered them in cold blood. With satanic rage they were not satisfied with murder, but shot to dismember and disfigure ensuring that the brains of their victims spilled far away from their craniums. These Salvadorian theologians had worked tirelessly to reconcile government and guerrilla, laying their lives on the altar of peace and justice. With sorrow I am forced to recognise that the bullets which blew these brains apart were supported by millions of conservative North American Evangelicals, evangelised by "successful" methods which some in Latin America wish to copy to fill their temples like those in North America.

Dietrich Bonhoeffer, the great Christian martyr murdered by Adolf Hitler two weeks before the end of the Second World War, realised at a certain point in his pastoral ministry that the Lord would call him to account for his historical faithfulness at a critical moment in his nation's history. He had always understood that he would be held accountable for his doctrinal faithfulness, his personal life, and his pastoral work. However, one day he realised that the Lord would judge him for his historical faithfulness when faced with Nazi atrocities in his days, for what he did and did not do in favour of the victims of injustice, for his own part in influencing the course of his nation's history and the world. Bonhoeffer gave his life out of faithfulness to the Gospel. God will also call us to account with regards to our faithfulness when faced with the injustices and atrocities in Latin America.

As evangelicals we need to pay attention to the solemn words of Matthew 7:21-23, especially as we examine our methods of evangelisation.

> Not everyone who says to me, 'Lord, Lord,' will enter the kingdom of heaven, but only the one who does the will of my Father in heaven. On that day many will say to me, 'Lord, Lord, did we not prophesy in your name, and cast out demons in your name, and do many deeds of power in your name?' Then I will declare to them, 'I never knew you; go away from me, you evildoers.'

Such strong words call North American and Latin American evangelicals to look deeply into our consciences. Are we those who, saved by grace, are living our lives in obedience to our Father's will in all areas of our life? Or would Christ have to unmask our religious façade to shame us concerning the evil in our individual and communal lives? Hopefully, we are not fooling ourselves with the misplaced confidence of those who said "Lord, Lord"!

Examining ourselves as evangelicals, we need to ask ourselves if the following contemporary version could apply to us:

> Lord, Lord, you know that I accepted you at the Aztec Stadium or at Madison Square Garden. Lord, Lord, I have been a member, in full fellowship, of the largest megachurch in my country. Lord, Lord, we do not smoke or drink alcohol, we go to all the services and tithe. And the Lord will say to us,
>
> "Go away from me, you evil doers. While you tithed your salaries, you applauded while the government decimated whole populations. You, Salvadorian evangelical,

> slept peacefully at night while the government systematically tortured its victims. You, Guatemalan evangelical, you chose to ignore while your government, year after year, massacred thousands of your indigenous brothers and sisters, peasants, students, and trade unionists. Latin American evangelicals, you refused to struggle for a more just economy which could save the lives of millions who died of hunger without Christ. Millions died without medical assistance, and you voted for cuts to public health. Worse of all, you had the audacity to call yourselves evangelicals. You called me Lord, but refused to obey me, you called me Master but did not listen to me, you called me the way, but refused to walk with me. Go away from me you evildoers."

Dear brothers and sisters, let us once more dedicate our whole being to Christ as Lord of our whole life. Let us dedicate ourselves like never before to the valuable task of an authentic and integral evangelisation. "All the gospel," according to the full biblical message, "to all the peoples," starting with those peoples within our nations and reaching the ends of the earth because our God is Creator and Lord of the whole earth: "From Latin America" without importing methods which have no roots in the gospel, nor in the Scriptures, nor in our Latin American realities. I pray that God can convert us from importers into exporters, and that from Latin America biblical and integral methods of evangelisation can reach other continents for the glory of our beloved Lord and Saviour Jesus Christ. Let us declare in our own, authentic voice that "we are not ashamed of the gospel; it is the power of God for salvation to everyone who has faith." Amen, our Lord, let it be so!

Conclusion

Our research has revealed that throughout Scripture creation is a constant, central and important theme. Therefore, it seems obvious that creation theology should play a similar and proportional role in our contemporary evangelical theology. Nonetheless, apart from the controversies against evolution, most of Protestantism seems to have forgotten the theme of creation.

We have also seen that throughout the Bible creation theology is intricately linked to the message of salvation. In biblical thought creation is not understood separately from salvation and salvation is not understood separately from creation. Thus, creation theology is essential for our faithful understanding of both the gospel and the mission of the church. We cannot understand salvation and mission biblically if we separate them from creation.

We have also seen that the biblical witness repeatedly affirms, from the first chapter of Genesis, that creation is good. The whole Bible breathes the joy of the good creation and God invites us, in the present, to "be glad and rejoice forever in what I am creating" (Isaiah 65:18).

Our salvation, rather than being a rejection of material reality, is in all its dimensions a new affirmation of God's good creation. In the incarnation God makes himself matter in an unprecedented manner, lives a human life and achieves our eternal salvation in a human body. He resurrects from death in a tangible and visible body which can be seen and touched by his disciples with whom he walks and even eats. Through faith he also makes us a new creation. We await the resurrection of our bodies, following the model of his physical resurrection. Meanwhile, we need to present our bodies in a living, pleasing sacrifice to God (Romans 12:1ff), feeding our Christian life with the material elements of bread and wine in communion. All this affirms the goodness of the created order. The Anglican theologian William Temple was right to declare that Christianity is the most materialistic religion of human history.

Throughout these chapters we have tried to portray biblical teaching on creation as thoroughly and faithfully as possible. We also hope to have highlighted some issues for a new focus on the gospel, evangelisation and the mission of the church, aligned with the biblical meaning of creation.

The following saying, attributed to Saint Augustine, is an apt summary of what we have been arguing: "there is no health for those who despise God's creation."

Studying the relationship between creation and salvation fills us with a sense of the Creator's glory and the greatness of his double work of creation and salvation. From the cosmic dimensions of creation we start to discover that we have had an extremely reduced understanding of "so great a salvation" (Hebrews 2:3). Creation theology and other aspects of biblical thought cry out "Salvation is much, much more than what you have understood! Open your eyes to the greatness of salvation: the width, breadth, depth and height of God's love."

Bibliography

ANDERSON, Bernard W., *Understanding Old Testament*, Prentice-Hall, Englewood Cliffs, 1957.

______. *Creation in the Old Testament*. Philadelphia: Fortress, 1984.

______. *Creation and Chaos*. Philadelphia: Fortress, 1987.

AUZOU, Georges. *En un principio Dios creó al mundo*. Navarra: Estella, 1982.

BARBAGLIO, G y G. Colombo. *Nuevo diccionario de teología*. Madrid: Cristiandad, 1977.

BARTH, Karl. *Church dogmatics*. Grand Rapids: Eerdmans, III/1, 1958; III/2, 1960; IV/1, 1956.

BEKER, J. Christian. *Paul's apocaliptic gospel. The coming triumph of God*. Philadelphia: Fortress, 1982.

BERKHOF, Hendrikus. *Christian faith*. Grand Rapids: Eerdmans, 1980.

BLACK, Matthew & ROWLEY, H.H. *Peake's Commentary on the Bible*. London: Nelson, 1962.

BOFF, Leonardo. *San Francisco de Asís: ternura y vigor*. Santander: Sal Terrae, 1982.

BOWMAN, John Wick. *Prophetic Realism and the Gospel: A Preface to Biblical Theology*. Philadelphie: Westminster, 1955.

BRENEMAN, Mervin. La misión en el Antiguo Testamento. *Misión*, no. 1, Marzo a junio de 1982a.

______. Génesis 1-3: La base de la misión. *Misión*, no. 2, julio a setiembre, 1982b.

______. Los profetas y las naciones. *Misión*, no.8, marzo de 1984.

______. La naturaleza de la misión. *Misión*, no. 17, junio de 1986.

BRUCE, F.F. 1 y 2 Tesalonicenses. In: GUTHRIE, D. (ed.) *Nuevo comentario bíblico*. El Paso: Casa Bautista de Publicaciones, 1977.

CORDERO, Maximilano G. Isaías. *Biblia Comentada III*. Madrid: BAC, 1967.

______. *Teología de la Biblia*. Madrid: BAC, 1970.

CORTÉS, Benjamín et all. *Los gemidos de la creación: ecología y teología desde la nueva Nicaragua*. Managua: CIEETS, 1988.

CROATTO, Severino. *El hombre en el mundo1*. Buenos Aires: La Aurora, 1974.

DEIROS, Pablo. *Santiago y Judas: Comentario bíblico hispanoamericano*. Miami: Caribe, 1992.

DE SOLA, Abraham (ed.). *The forms of prayer*. Philadelphia: Sherman, 1877.

DRIVER, John. *Pueblo o la imagen de Dios*. Guatemala: Clara | Bogotá: Semilla, 1991.

EICHRODT, Walter. *Teología del Antiguo Testamento.* Madrid: Cristiandad, 1975.

ELSHTAIN, Jean Bethke. *The Christian Century*, Chicago, 15 January 1992.

FOERSTER, Werner. 'Ktízo'. In: *Theological Dictionary of the New Testament.* Grand Rapids: Eerdmans, 1965.

FRICK, R. *Die Religion in Geschichte und Gegenwart*[1]. Tübingen, 1957.

FUNG, Raymond. *The Isaiah Vision.* Geneva: CMI, 1992.

GLETZER, Nahum. *Hammer on the rock: A Midrash reader.* Nova Iorque: Schocken, 1962.

GRABNER-MAIDER, Anton. *La Biblia y nuestro lenguaje.* Barcelona: Herder, 1975.

GUELLAY, Robert. *La creación.* Barcelona: Herder, 1979.

HEDSTROM, Ingemar. *Somos parte de un gran equilibrio: la crisis ecológica en Centroamérica.* San José: DEI, 1985.

______. *¿Volverán las golondrinas? La reintegración de la creación desde una perspectiva latinoamericana.* San José: DEI, 1988.

HESCHEL, Abraham. *Los profetas.* Buenos Aires: Paidós, 1973.

HOFFMANN, Arzemiro. La creación gime y se angustia... la responsabilidad ecológica de los cristianos. In: Steuernagel, Valdir (ed.). *La misión de la iglesia: una visión panorámica.* San José: Visión Mundial, 1992.

JACOB, Edmond. *Teología del Antiguo Testamento.* Madrid: Marova, 1969.

JENNI, Ernst & WESTERMANN, Claus. *Diccionario teológico manual del Antiguo Testamento.* Madrid: Cristiandad, 1969.

KLINE, Meredith. Génesis. In: Guthrie, D. *Nuevo comentario bíblico.* El Paso: Casa Bautista de Publicaciones, 1977.

LÉON-DUFOUR, Xavier. *Vocabulario de teología biblica.* Barcelona: Herder, 1965.

LIGHTFOOT, J.B. *Saint Paul's Epistles to the Colossians and to Philemon.* London: Macmillan, 1886.

LOSADA, L. S. & ANGULO, J. M. *La restauración de todas las cosas: misiología bíblica integral.* Guatemala: Semilla | Bogotá: Clara, 1992.

MACHEN, J.G. Gresham. *Christianity and liberalism.* Grand Rapids: Eerdmans, 1946.

MANSON, T.W. *The teaching of Jesus.* Cambridge: University of Cambridge, 1931.

MOLTMANN, Jürgen. *Teología de la esperanza.* Salamanca: Sígueme, 1969.

______. *El futuro de la creación.* Salamanca: Sígueme, 1979.

______. *Dios en la creación.* Salamanca: Sígueme, 1987.

MORIARTY, F.L. Isaías. In: *La Sagrada Escritura. Texto y comentario Antiguo Testamento V.* Madrid: BAC, 1961.

NEWBIGIN, Leslie. *Pecado y salvación.* Buenos Aires: Methopress, 1964.

PADILLA, René. *Misión Integral. Ensayos sobre el Reino y la Iglesia.* Buenos Aires: Nueva Creación, 1986.

PERKINS, John. *Justicia para todos.* Grand Rapids: Nueva Creación, 1988.

PETERSON, Eugene. *Reversed Thunder.* New York: Harper & Row, 1988.

RAHNER, Karl. Novísimos. In: *Sacramentum Mundi IV.* Barcelona: Herder, 1984.

RAMM, Bernard. "The Theology of Evangelism", *Occasional Papers*, Institute of Youth Ministries | Fuller Theological Seminary, 1978

RUIZ DE LA PEÑA, Juan L.. *Teología de la creación.* Santander: Sal Terrae, 1986.

SCHILLEBEECX, Edward. *Cristo y los cristianos: gracia y liberación.* Madrid: Cristiandad, 1977.

SCHÖKEL, L. A. & DÍAZ, J.L.S. *Profetas.* Madrid: Cristiandad, 1979.

SCHRENK, G. Dikaiosúne. In: *Theological Dictionary of the New Testament II.* Grand Rapids: Eerdmans, 1965.

SOBOTTKA, Emil. Hasta los demonios creen, pero su fe está muerta. In: Steuernagel, Valdir (ed.). *La misión de la iglesia: una visión panorámica.* San José: Visión Mundial, 1992.

STAM, Juan. La historia de la salvación y la misión integral de la iglesia. In: Steuernagel, Valdir (ed.). *La misión de la iglesia: una visión panorámica.* San José: Visión Mundial, 1992.

STRACHAN, Kenneth. *El llamado ineludible.* San José: Caribe, 1969.

TRIGO, Pedro. Creación y mundo material. In: Ellacuría, Ignacio y Sobrino, Jon (eds.) *Mysterium liberationis.* San Salvador: UCA Editores, 1990.

VAN IMSCHOOT, P. *Teología del Antiguo Testamento.* Madrid: Fax, 1966.

VON RAD, Gerhard. *Teología del Antiguo Testamento.* Salamanca: Sígueme, vol.1, 1972.

______. *Teología del Antiguo Testamento.* Salamanca: Sígueme, vol.2, 1973.

______. *Estudios sobre el Antiguo Testamento.* Salamanca: Sígueme, 1976.

______. *Génesis.* Salamanca: Sígueme, 1982.

WHITE, Lynn. "The historical roots of our ecological crisis", *Science* 155, March 10th, 1967; 156, May 12th, 1967.

WILKINSON, Loren (ed.). *Earthkeeping: Christian stewardships of natural resources.* Grand Rapids: Eerdmans, 1980.

YODER, John Howard et all. *La irrupción del* shalom: *en el pueblo de Dios se ha iniciado la renovación del mundo.* México: Servicio Paz y Justicia, 1992.

ZIMMERLI, W. *Manual de teología del Antiguo Testamento.* Madrid: Cristiandad, 1980.